Education and Politics
in the 1990s:
Conflict or Consensus?

Education and Politics in the 1990s:
Conflict or Consensus?

Denis Lawton

 The Falmer Press

(A member of the Taylor & Francis Group)
London • Washington, D.C.

UK	The Falmer Press, 4 John St., London, WC1N 2ET
USA	The Falmer Press, Taylor & Francis Inc., 1900 Frost Road, 101, Bristol, PA 19007

First published 1992   Reprinted 1994

Library of Congress Cataloging-in-Publication data are available on request

A catalogue record for this book is available from the British Library

ISBN 0 75070 078 5 cased
ISBN 0 75070 079 3 paperback

Set in 12/14pt Bembo by
Graphicraft Typesetters Ltd., Hong Kong

Printed in Great Britain by Burgess Science Press, Basingstoke on paper which has a specified pH value on final paper manufacture of not less than 7.5 and is therefore 'acid free'.

Contents

List of Abbreviations

AERA	American Educational Research Association
APS	Assisted Places Scheme
APU	Assessment of Performance Unit
ASI	Adam Smith Institute
BERA	British Educational Research Association
BJES	British Journal of Educational Studies
CNACE	Conservative National Advisory Committee on Education
CPC	Conservative Political Centre
CPES	Council for the Preservation of Educational Standards (later NCES)
CPG	Conservative Philosophy Group
CPS	Centre for Policy Studies
CPVE	Certificate of Pre-Vocational Education
CQS	Critical Quarterly Society
CSE	Certificate of Secondary Education
DES	Department of Education and Science
ESRC	Economic and Social Research Council
FEVER	Friends of the Education Voucher Experiment in Representative Regions
GCE	General Certificate of Education
GCSE	General Certificate of Secondary Education
HMI	Her Majesty's Inspectorate
IEA	Institute of Economic Affairs
ILEA	Inner London Education Authority
IPPR	Institute of Public Policy Research

ISJC	Independent Schools Joint Committee
KS1	Key Stage 1 (of National Curriculum)
LEA	Local Education Authorities
MSC	Manpower Services Commission
NCC	National Curriculum Council
NCES	National Council for Educational Standards
NFER	National Foundation for Educational Research
NIESR	National Institute for Economic and Social Research
NUT	National Union of Teachers
OECD	Organisation for Economic Cooperation and Development
SAT	Standard Assessment Task (for National Curriculum)
SAU	Social Affairs Unit
SEAC	School Examinations and Assessment Council
SEC	Secondary Examinations Council
SG	Salisbury Group
SHA	Secondary Heads Association
TA	Teacher Assessment
TES	Times Educational Supplement
TVEI	Technical and Vocational Education Initiative

The Purpose of the Book

In September 1989 I stepped down as Director of the Institute of Education, University of London. I had asked to be relieved of my administrative duties so that I would have time to reflect on what was happening at a crucial time for education, and to look at possible future developments. Kenneth Baker's Education Reform Act (1988) was beginning to take effect in a variety of ways; I spent the years 1989 and 1990 partly looking at the educational changes brought about during the Thatcher years (1979–90) and partly reading about the 'New Right': its origins, its nature and what various people thought might happen next.

During the course of 1989 and 1990, I also had the opportunity of visiting a number of other countries and talking to visitors from a wide variety of education systems. It was remarkable that so many of these countries, whatever the political complexion of the government in power, were undertaking 'reforms' which in England were described as 'Thatcherite'. Clearly something was happening politically and educationally on more than a national scale.

Before the end of that period, two other changes took place. First, in Eastern Europe communist regimes began to collapse or change dramatically — Ralf Dahrendorf wrote perceptively about 'The Strange Death of Socialism' (1990); second, in November 1990, Margaret Thatcher resigned as Prime Minister, but it was not clear whether this would be the end of 'Thatcherism'. These events caused many people to rethink political views, and caused me to reconsider the relation between politics and education.

The result is this book which is based on a number of assumptions:

(i) that education is inevitably political, in the sense that the aims of education will be related to ideology of some kind;

(ii) but there are dangers for the order and continuity of the education system if education becomes overtly and aggressively *party* political;

(iii) the Thatcher government from 1979 to 90 took education perilously close to that point;

(iv) after Margaret Thatcher's resignation, despite some signs of a shift away from individualism, the New Right policies in education continued, but perhaps with less conviction;

(v) we should now be planning for educational consensus, whatever the next government might be.

Before beginning to discuss the possibility or desirability of that kind of 'planning for consensus', it may be helpful to examine the nature of the ideological differences about education between the two major parties in order to explore what kind of consensus might be possible. One of the features of educational development in this country is that until recently (i.e., the 1970s) there was surprisingly little open ideological conflict on education, and, some would say, not much by way of policy either! Perhaps the way towards a new consensus will be not to ignore political/ideological differences but to recognize their existence whilst trying to get beyond them.

The plan of the book will be to discuss in chapter 1 the relation between politics, ideology and the education system of England and Wales. Chapter 2 will then trace the development of a Labour Party ideology on education with particular reference to the period 1944–1988. In chapter 3 I will cover the same period but from the point of view of the development of Conservative Party ideologies and policies. Part of the purpose of chapters 2 and 3 will be to show that until quite recently (1979), although there were differences between the two parties, they did not prevent consensus planning. Chapter 4 will look specifically at the development of a changing Conservative ideology in the 1980s, and in particular at its expression in the Education Reform Act (ERA) of 1988, and the increase in ideological conflict about education. Chapter 5 will look briefly at the events in education from 1988–1991. Chapter 6 will analyze the complex issue of 'choice' in education — in the context of both a planned system and its free market alternatives. Finally, chapters 7 and 8 will map out a possible consensus policy for education in the 1990s.

Denis Lawton
November 1991

Chapter 1

Politics, Ideology and Education

The Old Testament prophets did not say 'Brothers I want a consensus'. They said: 'This is my faith, this is what I passionately believe. If you believe it too, then come with me.' (Margaret Thatcher (1979) quoted by Gamble (1988)

A good deal has been written about the New Right, Reaganomics in the USA, and Thatcherism in the UK, but comparatively little has been written about the New Right and education. In this chapter I want to try to fill that gap by exploring the concept ideology and the ideas of the New Right on education.

Whatever one's views about political and educational events since 1979, it is difficult to disagree with the view that education in England will never be the same again. In education — as with other aspects of social life — the policies pursued since the Conservative victory in 1979 have brought about some changes which are irreversible. One of the problems for those who have come after Margaret Thatcher is to decide exactly what they should try to reverse and what might provide a platform for further development. At the time of writing (August 1991) it was too soon to decide whether John Major as Prime Minister would continue the Thatcher tradition in education or would embark on radical new ventures. The only clues were his early statements about the desirability of a 'classless society', his speech to the Young Conservatives in February 1991 and his July 1991 address on education to the Centre for Policy Studies in which he indicated that he would give the highest priority to education and training.

But what kind of education? It seems likely that some aspects of Thatcherism will continue, at least in the short term. It is, therefore, important to analyze the impact of New Right ideas on education, for their future relevance as well as out of purely historical interest.

Some educationists, whilst disapproving of much that happened during the period 1979 to 1990, would be willing to acknowledge that all was not well with the education service in the 1970s and that in the 1980s education was at least submitted to radical review. But another way of looking at those years would suggest that some policies have come perilously close to destroying the DES/LEA partnership system altogether.

The New Right and Thatcherism

Several complete books have been written on this question (for example, Gamble, 1988; Skidelsky, 1988; Kavanagh, 1987; Kavanagh and Seldon, 1989; Hall and Jacques, 1983. Many of them, correctly in my view, wish to distinguish between the emergence (or re-emergence) of certain right-wing policies, and the particular style and personality of Margaret Thatcher. This is important but not always easy.

Another aspect of the problem of analyzing Thatcherism is that it combined features of neo-liberal libertarianism as well as neo-conservative 'cultural rightism' which are by no means completely compatible, and are seen by some to be contradictory. Yet another feature of Thatcherism was that it attempted to generalize the laissez-faire economic doctrines of the neo-liberals into the whole of social life under the guise of another ideology — individualism.

It is probably safe to say that most of these doctrines of the 'New Right' would have become part of the political debate of the 1980s without Margaret Thatcher as Prime Minister. They were part of worldwide changes in the political debate, but she added a style of leadership and public argument which increased the impact and influence of those doctrines.

What then is, or was, Thatcherism? And what has been its effect on education? Some writers, for example, Kavanagh (1987) and Skidelsky (1988) have examined Thatcherism in the context of the political failures (Labour and Conservative) of the 1960s and 1970s. Part of Margaret Thatcher's appeal may have been that she offered to lead the Conservative Party (and the country) away from the 'consensus politics' which had failed to work for Wilson, Heath or Callaghan. Hence the quotation which heads this chapter. But that cannot be the whole truth: the evidence of public opinion polls and analyses of popular values indicate a lack of wholesale support for the more extreme aspects of Thatcherism.

The consensus approach which Margaret Thatcher disliked involved trying to make an ailing mixed economy work, and was based on Keynesian economics as well as guaranteed support for the welfare state — including education. We shall see, in some detail in chapter 3, that the apparent consensus between Crosland and Boyle on education policies was encountering more and more criticism from within the Conservative Party in the late 1960s and 1970s. This could be seen as part of a much wider, to some extent international, reaction against collectivism — or at least against some practices of collectivist administrations.

Let us then return to the twin New Right ideological bases of Thatcherism: neo-liberal economic theories and neo-conservatism, which are philosophically quite distinct.

Neo-liberalism derives from the ideas of the eighteenth century classical economist, Adam Smith. Some like Hahn (1988) would say on an over simplification or misinterpretation of Smith. The major modern exponent of the free market is however the Austrian economist Hayek who condemned socialism as *The Road to Serfdom* (1944) and saw collectivist ideas and practices as a threat to freedom and prosperity. It was Hayek who in 1947 founded an international society devoted to the preservation of the non-socialist liberal order (later called the Mount Pelerin Society, after its first meeting place in Switzerland). Many English right-wing economists have been members of, and contributed to, the discussions of the Society. A recurring theme in Hayek's work has been the idea that collectivist social planning is doomed to failure because society is so complex and the 'facts' that planners deal with are not concrete, but are based on human behaviour and relationships which are unpredictable. Hence, according to Hayek, the superiority of the free market over any kind of planning for full employment, a welfare state, economic targets and redistribution of income. The market mechanism is superior to all planning because it works automatically with a beautiful simplicity — if you leave it alone. The 'selfish' acts of individuals end up by being for the good of society as a whole.

There is a theory behind this optimistic faith. Hayek argues that the classic distinction between 'natural' and 'artificial' is false because there is a third category of 'social' which includes human institutions that have evolved rather than been consciously planned. Language would be a good example of the social category, law would be another, and in some societies, the notion of the market as a means of organizing the production and exchange of goods and services. To illustrate his faith in the social benefits arising out of selfish individual acts, Hayek uses the example of a footpath: an individual will tend to choose to walk in someone else's tracks, not with the intention of helping to create a footpath, but simply because it is easier to walk where someone else has already trodden down the plants. But the beneficial, unintended result is — eventually — a footpath for the whole community! However, if we try to *plan*, we run the risk of believing that one individual (or a group of planners) can understand detailed human needs better than a system developed unconsciously over many generations. We should beware of tampering with an established social institution such as the market which works automatically and is not amenable to improvement because it is already a perfect mechanism based on the freedom of individuals making their own decisions rather than being told what is good for them. (Hayek does not say what a group of individuals should do who, seeing the benefit of a footpath, decide they would like a bridge.)

Part of Hayek's faith in the free market is based on a simple belief (which, ironically, he shares with Marx) that the *economic* relationship between individuals is the dominant social relationship: social theory should be based on this 'fact' not on the desire to do good, to be generous or to put right any injustices. The price mechanism is superior to those sentiments — it is the perfect information system for the whole society, ensuring by automatic competition low costs and efficiency. Such supply and demand information could never be known to any central planning bureaucracy. The free market mechanism is superior to planning both in terms of efficiency and in terms of individual freedom. Economic freedom means social freedom. There will, of course, be 'winners and losers' as the result of the market. But we should be careful not to introduce ideas of fairness or social justice into the formula. In a free market economy there will, for example, be occasions when a poor individual will die because he cannot afford expensive drugs or an operation, but that is not unfair or unjust — it is only a bit of bad luck:

> To discover the meaning of what is called 'social justice' has been one of my chief preoccupations for more than ten years. I have failed in this endeavour — or rather, have reached the conclusion that, with reference to a society of free men, the phrase has no meaning whatever. (Hayek, 1978, p. 57. See also Hayek, 1976)

If an individual contracts a fatal disease, this may be, according to Hayek, unfortunate, but it is not meaningful to say that it is 'unjust' because justice is a moral concept necessarily involving human motivation and behaviour: it is unjust for an individual to steal from another, but it cannot be unjust for an individual to be ill or poor or badly housed — they are simply the losers in a game of chance. (Hayek criticizes socialists for the mistaken concept of social justice, but ignores the traditional Christian doctrine about the existence of sins of omission as well as sins of commission — that is, that it is a sin to fail to give charity to the poor as well as to steal from the rich.)

Hayek and his followers insist that 'social justice' or 'redistributive justice' is not only meaningless but is fraudulent and harmful to freedom. The financial rewards bestowed upon individuals by the market will, in general, be good indicators of their 'contribution' (apart from luck), but will not necessarily fit in with any collectivist notion of social justice, need or merit. Hayek does not, however, go as far as some libertarians such as the American philosopher Nozick (1974) who claims that taxation is a combination of theft and slavery; Hayek acknowledges the need for a minimum state to ensure that the economic game is played fairly. Thus some coercion may be necessary, but it should be as little as possible. An army to guard against foreign interference and a police force to preserve traditional law and order would be permitted, but much of the collectivist welfare state would have to go.

I have dealt with Hayek at some length because his ideas are directly relevant to some aspects of economic Thatcherism and indirectly relevant to some New Right views on education. It is quite easy to see links between Hayek's views and the public statements of Margaret Thatcher, and, in particular, of her one-time mentor, Keith Joseph:

> The blind, unplanned, uncoordinated wisdom of the market . . .is overwhelmingly superior to the well-researched, rational, systematic, well-meaning, cooperative, science-based, forward-looking, statistically respectable plans of government. . .The market system is the greatest generator of national wealth known to mankind: coordinating and fulfilling the diverse needs of countless individuals in a way which no human mind or minds could ever compre-hend, without coercion, without direction, without bureau-cratic interference. (Joseph, 1976)

As we shall see, the problem of reconciling such Hayekian views with the task of making a collectivist state education system work, proved difficult for Joseph when he became Secretary of State for Education and Science. In addition, several Conservative Party education advisers have been influenced by Hayek, for example, Oliver Letwin (1988) and Stuart Sexton, arguably the major architect of education policy in the Thatcher years, is a consistent advocate of bringing education more into line with the free market (see chapter 3). As we shall also see, some aspects of ERA (1988) were the result of right-wing interventions from the free market side of the Conservative Party. Hugo Young (1989) suggests that Margaret Thatcher had read *The Road to Serfdom* when she was an Oxford undergraduate, but that she did not get to grips with Hayek's other work until the 1970s. Other influences were im-portant, including that of Keith Joseph, and, indirectly, Milton Friedman.

So much for the neo-liberal ideological side of Thatcherism.

I will now deal more briefly with the neo-Conservative ideology and its influence on the New Right and education policies. Neo-liberal Hayekian thinking is optimistic in believing that human selfishness is not a problem because it is eventually transformed into a public good. (A view derived from Leibniz and satirised by Voltaire in *Candide* as 'all is for the best in the best of all possible worlds'); neo-Conservative thinking, on the other hand, has a more pessimistic view of society derived from Hobbes's vision of human interaction as 'nasty, brutish and short' unless human nature could be tightly constrained by social rules. This view can be seen in the context of the history of the Conservative Party in some of the writings of Edmund Burke and in the paternalist doctrine of the strong state to control evil (and sometimes to protect the weak). 'Custom', 'tradition' and 'order' are the key words in this conception of the state and political theory. One version of this view assumes that tradition and order are essential, but claims that Conservatives are non-ideological and pragmatic. This has tended to be the attitude of some anti-Thatcherites in the Conservative Party such as James Prior, Sir Ian Gilmour and others who left her Cabinet.

The 1980s version of this Conservative tradition has been provided, above all, by Roger Scruton. In his book *The Meaning of Conservatism* (1980) Scruton defines the traditionalist character of Conservative political doctrine, and in other publications such as *The Salisbury Review*, which he edits, he brings these traditional views to bear on problems of modern English society such as gender, race and education.

It is this strand of Conservative thinking which is frequently behind education publications of the Hillgate Group making pronouncements on the curriculum (*The Reform of British Education*, 1987), teacher training (*Learning to Teach*, 1989) and the dangers of left-wing indoctrination (Scruton *et al*, 1985). I shall want to refer to these later: at this stage I would simply like to note that whereas the neo-liberals tend to talk about choice, competition and the market in education, the neo-Conservatives are more likely to advocate traditional values, traditional subjects, and less educational theory in the training of teachers, but greater immersion into the traditional values of good schools. The mixture of neo-liberal and neo-conservative doctrines is uncomfortable,

7

although some individuals have managed to write for both groups, for example Dennis O'Keeffe who wrote *The Wayward Elite* (1990) for the Adam Smith Institute having previously collaborated with Scruton (1985) on *Education and Indoctrination*.

Andrew Gamble (1988) argues that Thatcherism is a combination of the two traditions I have described above, which Gamble refers to as 'the free economy and the strong state'. Margaret Thatcher managed to square the circle by ensuring that 'rolling back the state' meant a reduction in the scope of government but not a diminution in its strength. Less government need not mean weak government.

Gamble sees Thatcherism as a particular manifestation of New Right politics which emerged in the 1970s in response to the world recession, the exhaustion of Fordism as a regime of accumulation and the breakdown of American hegemony. In Britain Thatcherism had the peculiar national characterization derived partly from the crisis of state authority in the mid-1970s — and not least the failure of Heath to win the 1974 election with a 'Who governs Britain?', anti-union campaign. Denis Healey (1989) in his autobiography suggests:

> Mrs. Thatcher did not create what is now called 'Thatcherism' out of the blue. She gave expression to feelings which were already colouring public opinion on both sides of the Atlantic; the attitudes she rejected had already begun to lose their appeal. Underlying all these changes was a reaction throughout the developed world against the permissiveness of the 60s, which had found its most extreme form in the culture of the Hippy generation. Ordinary people longed for a return to order, to the family values which used to provide a moral framework for individual behaviour. They were not prepared to believe patriotism was evil, that all authority was bad, that every leader was bound to betray his cause, that the pursuit of excellence was what the New Left regarded as the worst of all possible vices — 'elitism'. Ronald Reagan represented this backlash in the US, as Margaret Thatcher did in Britain; in this sense their victories were a triumph for traditional bourgeois values.

Thatcherism began to develop as a serious ideology after she became Leader of the Opposition in 1975. But Gamble (1988) warns us that Thatcherism is an ambiguous and misleading concept:

> Critics of the concept argue that it is misleading firstly because it directs attention to what is trivial and relatively unimportant, and secondly because it attributes to the actions and ideas of the Thatcher government a degree of coherence and purpose that does not exist. (p. 21)

This is particularly true of education policies. It is difficult to see educational change since 1979 as a coherent expression of any ideology. Yet many developments have taken place in education, and it is necessary to try to assess their significance and importance in the longer term. It is also important not to underestimate the moral dimension of popular thinking reflected in Thatcherism, as Denis Healey (1989) has pointed out:

> Combined with this backlash against the permissive society — and in some ways at odds with it — was a widespread desire to reduce the role of the government in economic and social affairs. There was a longing to make people more self-reliant, and less dependent on state assistance which was granted unconditionally to anyone in need. Too many people were seen as 'scrounging' on the welfare state. As confidence in the government diminished, faith in the magic of the market-place increased. The pursuit of personal gain was seen once again as the most reliable motive force not only in economic life, but in many other areas of society. (p. 486)

In education, this moral backlash against 'permissiveness' was, as we shall see in chapter 3, linked to questions of standards in schools and universities, and to the feeling that lower standards were related to 'progressive methods'.

But why should such views be in any way connected with the political Left and Right, with Labour and Conservative parties? Part of the answer is provided by the concept ideology.

The Meaning of Ideology

One of the problems about 'ideology' is that the word is used in different ways by various writers (or even by the same writer at different times). The second difficulty is that the word is used at various levels of generality — ranging from descriptions of the world view of a class or political movement (for example, bourgeois ideology), to more specific sets of beliefs or attitudes, (for example, how teachers envisage and justify their style of teaching).

The *Concise Oxford Dictionary* gives the following as the current meaning of ideology: 'manner of thinking characteristic of a class or individual, ideas at the basis of some economic or political theory or system'. I will be using 'ideology' in roughly that sense, except that I shall want to refine the concept by suggesting three levels of meaning, from the most general to the more specific. One further preliminary distinction might be helpful: when Marxists talk of 'bourgeois ideology' they imply that this ideology distorts the views of those who hold it. For some writers, ideology is always used with the implication of '*distorted* view of reality' (for example, Mannheim, 1936); others use the term more neutrally in the sense of any coherent (even if incorrect) set of beliefs and attitudes. There is, however, usually a hint in any discussion of ideology that to some extent it distorts perception because it represents an incomplete view of social reality.

I suggest that it is helpful to think of ideology and education as a set of three (overlapping) levels ranging from the very general (Level 1) to the specific (Level 3):

Level 1 (General/Political)

Individuals or groups may have general ideas and beliefs about human nature and society which then give rise to a range of more specific social and moral views and opinions, including, for example, the purpose of education, the functions of schooling and the appropriateness of teaching methods. 'Bourgeois ideology' and 'Marxist ideology' both encompass views on education, but education would seem to be less central than other beliefs. Both of those examples could be associated with political parties, but it should also be noted that it is *not* always possible to identify one ideology with any one political party: in the case of the Conservative Party and the Labour Party I shall later be suggesting that a mixture of ideologies is involved in each case, whereas a belief in Marxist ideology might be a prerequisite for membership of a Communist Party.

Level 2 (Interest Group Level)

At a more specific 'interest group' level we can identify ideologies associated with groups particularly concerned with education; for example, Raymond Williams (1961) talks of the influence on the curriculum of three 'groups' — the old humanists, the industrial trainers and the public educators (see below). I have also attempted to explain differences in attitude towards the national curriculum in terms of ideology at this level (Lawton, 1988).

Level 3 (Education/Teaching or Pedagogic Level)

At an even more specific level we have educational or teacher ideologies: how teachers envisage their role, the aims of education etc. Malcolm Skilbeck (1984) discussed three ideologies held by teachers   Classical Humanism, Progressivism and Reconstructionism — which were closely related to ideas about curriculum and teaching method (see below).

The assumption behind my three-level classification is that how anyone sees an educational issue or problem is not random or haphazard but is powerfully connected with other, frequently deep-rooted, sub-cultural and political beliefs, attitudes and values.

It may be useful to elaborate a little on each of those three levels.

Level 1 (The General or Political Level)

I have elsewhere (1989a) suggested that views about education can be polarized into two categories according to superordinate views about human nature and society. At one extreme we have the seventeenth century philosopher Hobbes (1588–1679) who was pessimistic about human nature, seeing human beings as essentially selfish and therefore needing 'society' to ensure order by means of social control. Without strong control from society, life would be 'nasty, brutish and short'. This view, I suggested above, also represents one important strand of traditional Conservatism.

At the other extreme the dominant thinking, especially in education, has been that of Rousseau. Rousseau's *Social Contract* (1762) begins with the much-quoted, but ambiguous statement: 'Men are born free, yet everywhere they are in chains'. Rousseau's view was that man was naturally good but corrupted by the *social institutions* imposed upon him. In *Emile* (1762) he attempted to apply this romanticism to education. He asserted that the task of education was not to encourage conformity to society's conventions and rules, but to enhance an individual's liberty and self-expression. Some kinds of Marxist thinking — but not all — make similar assumptions about good human begins being corrupted by capitalist institutions. This may be a partial explanation of the relation between political beliefs and educational practice. There is often an element of Rousseauism in the feelings of those who, dissatisfied with the injustices of the traditional social and political order, want radical change.

It is important to stress the polarity of these two positions; there are many positions between the two extremes. I would want to argue that human beings are a complex mixture of good and evil and would deny the simplistic opposition between human beings and society by asserting that individuals only become truly human by being part of some kind of community. And I think evidence could be mounted to give strong support to that 'moderate' position.

But for the moment let us remain with the two extremes in order to illustrate the differences very clearly. It is not surprising that those who have a pessimistic view of human nature would see the functions of the state in terms of law and order, protecting property and so on, and see education much more in terms of control, stressing obedience to authority, learning traditional kinds of knowledge by rote ('facts' in history and geography, for example).

At the other extreme, Rousseau's *Emile* tells the whole romantic story: the child must learn for him/herself rather than be told, self-expression is more important than knowing what others have invented, creativity is given high priority and so on. There is some truth in the suggestion that some colleges of education in the 1950s and 1960s placed considerable emphasis on Rousseau's philosophy. And from 1969 onwards, the Black Papers (Cox and Dyson, 1969 and 1970) consistently attacked what they regarded as the evil of exaggerated child-centred positions:

> A bankrupt and dangerous romanticism is at work, with its roots in the early nineteenth century or even before. 'The road of excess leads to the palace of wisdom' (Blake); 'I am certain of nothing but the holiness of the Heart's affections and the truths of Imagination' (Keats); 'Let Nature be your teacher' (Wordsworth). The essential notion is that men are born free and holy, but are crushed by false pressures from the social world. False laws and taboos, inequalities of class, privilege, wealth, colour and creed, are held responsible; the indictment is that all laws imposed on the self from outside contribute to 'man's inhumanity to man'. . . . Today, it has become almost a dogma with many educationists, and the unchallenged assumptions behind 'self-expression', 'self-fulfilment' as inalienable goods in themselves. (Dyson, 1969, in Cox and Dyson)

It would, however, be wrong to give the impression that this ideological polarization is just a matter of individual taste or personality, genetically determined. There are powerful social class factors operating as well: the rich and privileged have traditionally tended to be advocates of order and control without which they might be in danger of losing their property and privileges. This gives rise to social and ideological differences even to the meaning of such words as 'freedom' and 'rights': the Conservative tends to talk of 'freedom *to*' whereas the Left has associated liberty with 'freedom *from*' poverty, ignorance, ill-health etc. Similarly, there is a political distinction on the use of the word 'rights': rights of property as opposed to personal rights. The distinctions at party political level are probably complex mixtures of innate temperament, social class 'distortions', as well as other aspects of individual and group attitudes.

Level 2 (The Education Interest Group Level)

At the second level of ideological analysis I mentioned Raymond Williams' well known three-fold categorization. Williams sought to explain the differing attitudes to education which developed in the nineteenth century (and continued to be influential in the twentieth century) by postulating three ideologies: the old humanists, the industrial trainers and the public educators. This should not be seen as a contradiction of my Level 1 categorization but as a classification at a more specific or delicate level, still based partly on socioeconomic factors.

The old humanist view of education was associated with the upper classes, nobility and landed gentry, who saw the education of their own children in terms of character-building and learning gentlemanly behaviour: how to develop the superior style, tastes and manners appropriate for the ruling class. The classics had provided the perfect curriculum for that kind of education — a badge of rank as well as moral training. Education was necessarily an elitist activity.

The second group, the industrial trainers, (merchant, managerial and some professional classes) had the utilitarian aim of producing a well-trained and obedient workforce. Education was essentially useful, with practical objectives.

The third group, the public educators, had the ambition of educating the whole population for a democratic society. Their major aim was political or civic.

Williams' thesis was that universal education was achieved at the end of the nineteenth century by an uneasy, and unconscious, alliance between the industrial trainers and the public educators.

Another categorization of ideologies at this level is the one which I have previously used to explain differences in attitude towards the National Curriculum (Lawton, 1989a). These ideologies are more closely related to political parties, but not entirely, and there is an overlap in the middle. The four ideologies can be seen as a Right to Left continuum from Privatizers and Minimalists (on the right) to the Pluralists and the Comprehensive Planners on the left. More of that later.

Level 3 (The Pedagogical Level)

Finally, we have the third level of ideology — the teacher ideologies postulated by Skilbeck: the Classical Humanists, the Progressivists and the Reconstructionists. Note again that there is an overlap between the levels: Skilbeck's Classical Humanists have some similarity to Raymond Williams' old humanists, and Skilbeck's Progressivists and Reconstructionists would probably both fit into Williams' category of public educators. But Skilbeck was essentially referring to more specific beliefs, particularly those held by teachers about curriculum and pedagogy.

Ideology and Education in the 1980s and 1990s

How does all that kind of analysis relate to policies about education today?

Perhaps the greatest political/ideological difference in the 1980s was the question of planning versus laissez-faire or the free market: a simple left-right distinction. Some of those who favour the market rely on the neo-liberal theory that although individuals are intrinsically selfish, by happy chance, when they all seek to maximize their own interests by buying and selling in the market, a 'hidden hand' somehow transforms individual selfishness into public good (Hayek, 1976). I will not argue the contrary case at this stage, but it is necessary to make one observation: allowing the market to dominate favours the status quo where the strong and powerful — the privileged — get the best for their own children in education; one function of planning is that it tries to redress the balance by equalizing opportunities in education, but it does not always succeed. This is the obvious opposition between Right and Left in politics. The Right, with a vested interest in, or preference for, the status quo, favours traditional forms of education; the Left, perceiving society to be unjust and believing improvements to be possible, makes plans to achieve greater social justice, including equalizing educational opportunities.

The history of the Conservative Party and education is, as we shall see in chapter 3, complex. In broad-brush terms it is however true to say that there has been a gradual move away from the nineteenth century view that parents should pay for what they wanted and could afford, to the realization that some kind of state education system was necessary for a modern industrial society. These two ideas have tended to remain separate — i.e., a market (private) system for 'us' (the upper and upper-middle classes), and a state system for 'them'. The state system should provide good value for money ('sound and cheap'), but would not be good enough for 'us' (and it might not be desirable to mix the social classes anyway). Finally, especially since the 1944 Act, some Conservatives (but certainly not all) began to think in terms of a state system which would provide for all.

This sequence of three stages looked like an inevitable march of progress until the 1970s (and even more in the 1980s) when there was a backlash against state education. Some began to revert to a 'Privatizer' position, advocating the abolition of the state system and a return to market forces; others had specific complaints to make about the structure, content and style of state primary and comprehensive schools.

The history of the Labour Party and education can be summarized as a desire to plan to improve the life chances of working class boys (and, later, girls), but not quite knowing how to, and also being trapped within the deep structure of traditionalist beliefs about education in a society which was, and is, very conservative. They were also prevented from developing a coherent policy by the continued existence of conflicting opinions and even ideologies within the Party (see chapter 2).

It has also been suggested that there is a right wing interest in linking education to the needs of the labour market and therefore stressing skills. This may be true but superficial. At a less obvious level it might also be true that the Left are, with notable exceptions such as Gramsci, less interested in traditional disciplines, facts and skills, and more interested in imagination and creativity. Why? The right is concerned with facts and the status quo and wish to emphasize 'what is' rather than 'what might be', which is potentially subversive. In education, however, it is not a simple question of choosing either spelling or creative writing but of including both. Educational debate is rarely simple: part of the interest in the dispute about National Curriculum history, for example, was to analyze the opposition to the new history. Some traditionalists made an automatic response at the level of 'they should know the facts', but there were also more subtle concerns about content (for example, the need to include the history of the great British Empire), mixed up with the concern of professional historians that empathy teaching should not be exaggerated. It is a good illustration of the need for a well considered, intellectually justifiable consensus approach.

In an attempt to explain the political and ideological differences between individuals, groups and parties, I will now return to a fuller explanation of my own four category classification (at Level 2). It is useful to think of four ideologies (each of which may have a strong and a weak sub-category):

   (i)   the privatizers;
  (ii)   the minimalists;
 (iii)   the pluralists;
 (iv)   the comprehensive planners;

These four ideological positions do not correspond exactly to support for a political party. For example, a majority of Conservative voters probably favour comprehensive education — for practical rather than ideological reasons. But there is a clear move along a Right-Left continuum from the privatizers to the comprehensive planners. Each of the four ideologies has its origin in historical positions, but still exist as a coherent (but not necessarily valid) set of beliefs about contemporary education.

The privatizers would advocate leaving everything to the market. Parents should choose what they want and pay for what they can afford. After a long period when the privatizers' position was regarded as old-fashioned and eccentric, in the 1980s there was a renewal of interest in the view that education is essentially a private concern rather than something appropriate for government responsibility. An extreme version of this view would recommend privatizing all education from pre-school provision to university. *Our Schools* (Sexton, 1987) recommended privatizing schools; others have recommended the abolition of state subsidies for higher education. LEAs would be disbanded, all school would be run by Boards of Governors, private companies or groups of parents and teachers. Parents would have complete freedom to choose — moderated only by their ability to pay.

The ideological background for this view is laissez-faire capitalism with total reliance on market mechanisms to control the relation between supply and demand in education. Stuart Sexton and the Institute for Economic Affairs (IEA), as well as publications of the Adam Smith Institute and other neo-liberal groups, have argued along these lines, in more or less extreme versions. But not the Hillgate Group, Roger Scruton and the neo-conservatives who see education as too important a matter to be left to choice and the market.

Minimalists believe in a mixed economy in education. They accept that the state should provide basic schooling (as cheaply as possible), but parents must have the right and privilege of buying additional extras or of opting out of the state system altogether. The market is regarded as important for a free (capitalist) society, but should be moderated; in education they realize that the market itself cannot provide an adequate system for contemporary society.

This ideology leads to what Tawney (1931) criticized as a system run by those who felt that it was not good enough for their own children — one of the tragedies of British society. Some voucher systems could operate within this minimalist scenario; the Assisted Places Scheme is characteristic of the thinking behind minimalism (state schools are not really good enough for bright children). City technology colleges represent another example — providing a superior tier for a minority — as well as revealing hostility towards LEAs. Minimalists also tend to be segregators; they want to separate children according to social class, or supposed intellectual ability, perhaps even sex.

The political background to this ideology lies in the history of Tory paternalism — the idea that those who have the good fortune to be born into a position of wealth or rank have a duty to provide for the less fortunate (the deserving poor). Education must be provided for all, partly to train them for useful work, but also to provide for their social and moral well-being. But the education provided for the masses should be carefully controlled — not so good that it will give them ideas above their station — and not too expensive. An efficient system would also provide some opportunities for the very bright to join the ranks of their social superiors.

The pluralists would want to provide a state system so good that there would be little or no incentive to use independent schools. Their regard for individual freedom of choice would, however, not allow them to legislate private schools out of existence. Freedom to choose is more important than social justice or equality of opportunity. Socialists such as Tony Crosland came somewhat reluctantly to that point of view. The pragmatists in the group would argue that it would be impossible, even if desirable, to prevent parents sending their children to independent schools. It is alleged that some independent schools already have contingency plans to move to Ireland or elsewhere if they were threatened by punitive or preventative legislation.

Pluralists have invented such terms as 'parity of esteem' (for the different but equal types of secondary school within the tripartite system or, more recently, for post-16 academic and vocational provision). In the past they tended to oppose the idea of a centralized curriculum and consider that the curriculum is less important than organizational factors in providing good educational opportunities for all. They also tend to meritocratic beliefs in education, favouring the metaphor of 'the ladder of opportunity' rather than 'the broad highway'.

There are serious contradictions in this position: pluralism and 'parity' are difficult to reconcile, as are freedom and equality of opportunity, privilege and meritocracy. These contradictions, as we shall see in chapter 2, partly account for the past weakness of Labour Party education policies. The political ideology behind this view of education is Fabian or social democratic: a good society is a fair and free society, but when those two principles come into conflict freedom has to take precedence.

'*The comprehensive planners*' is a generic title for those who want high quality education for all and believe that this is best achieved by a unified, planned system. Comprehensive planners acknowledge that a watered-down version of pseudo-high culture curricula will not be appropriate for a society committed to genuine secondary education for all. They will also tend to criticize the grammar school curriculum for other reasons — epistemological, cultural and social as well as political.

The idea of a common or National Curriculum is commonplace elsewhere in the world but, at least since 1944, has been avoided in England where total state control of education continued to be regarded with suspicion. Raymond Williams (1961) was among the first to advocate a common curriculum for English schools. In 1973 I attempted to outline a common curriculum which would avoid the dangers and disadvantages of a uniform curriculum. Such attempts to devise a common curriculum rest on ideological assumptions about common culture and common schools, without denying individual differences and the need to provide for individual opportunities within a common plan. In practice, comprehensive schools have found it very difficult to escape completely from the 'dead hand' of the grammar school. The curricula of most comprehensive schools has tended to be a watered-down version of the grammar school curriculum for the more able pupils and a sad neglect of the needs of the less academic. There has also been a tendency to equate less academic with less intelligent, less worthy and less important. Comprehensive planners have therefore tended to place great emphasis on curriculum reform as a means of achieving a better and fairer education service.

Politics and Ideologies

I began this section by saying that there was no exact correspondence between the four ideologies outlined above and allegiance to the two main political parties. But it is quite clear that the privatizers and minimalists represent views which are predominantly found within Conservative ranks, whilst in the Labour Party the debate has tended to be between pluralists and comprehensive planners. As we shall see, however, there is also some overlap in the middle. But if there are any comprehensive planners in the Conservative Party they have kept their heads down in recent years. All four ideologies are backward-looking in the sense that they discuss education in terms of the 1944 Education Act rather than looking forward from the 1988 Education Act. A consensus approach will need to escape from all four ideologies and rethink the needs of the education service in the 1990s.

Chapters 2 and 3 will show how in both the Labour Party and the Conservative Party some ideological changes have taken place since 1944. Two aspects of those chapters may be surprising: first that policies on education have sometimes been so weak that they hardly existed; second, that until quite recently a broad consensus position in education was not only possible but normal — despite the considerable ideological differences between the two major parties.

After reviewing the development of educational policies in chapters 2 and 3, I will return in chapter 4 to a more detailed consideration of the ideological conflict which increased during the period 1979 to 1988 and reached a high point in the Education Reform Act (1988).

Chapter 2

Education, Ideology and the Labour Party

The gravest weakness of British Labour is one which it shares with the greater part of the world, including British capitalists. It is its lack of a creed. The Labour Party is hesitant in action because divided in mind. It does not achieve what it could, because it does not know what it wants. It frets out of office and fumbles in it, because it lacks the assurance either to wait or to strike. Being without clear convictions as to its own meaning and purpose, it is deprived of the dynamic which only convictions can supply. (Tawney, 1934)

By the time of the Butler Education Act (1944) the Labour Party had existed for less than forty years. During that period (1906–1944) the Party was divided on many issues, including education. Many writers have shown that the origins of the Labour Party were not socialist; Barker (1972) has also shown that as late as 1910 about half of the Parliamentary Labour Party had started as members of the Liberal Party and remained Liberals in their beliefs and attitudes when they transferred their allegiance to the Labour Party. For many the function of the Labour Party was to present a working class view on industry, employment, housing and social conditions rather than to represent a new ideology. For some, education was a higher priority than for others, and Parkinson (1970) has given some interesting examples of education policy being regarded as subservient to employment policy — some Labour members were doubtful about raising the school leaving age because this would reduce family incomes; others supported it because it would reduce unemployment. In 1947 C.V. Alexander argued that compulsory military service was a reasonable substitute for County Colleges (Dean, 1986).

There has been surprisingly little discussion of 'socialist education' throughout the history of the Party: utopian visions have been extremely rare, and the Labour Party has usually merely taken the existing education system and suggested minor adjustments to it in order to try to make it serve the interests of working class children more fairly. Tawney's *Secondary Education for All* (1922) came close to being an expression of desirable policy, but even that was essentially a criticism of the status quo and lacked the wholehearted support of the Party. When in 1923 the Labour Party formed its first minority government, C.P. Trevelyan, an ex-Liberal, became President of the Board of Education. He did not attempt to implement the 1922 document, but instead embarked upon a very modest programme of extending access to secondary schools. When the Labour Party fell in November 1924, Trevelyan made an interesting appeal for education to be kept out of politics. His view of consensus was that all parties should work for gradual expansion in education; this policy — or lack of policy — continued during the second Labour government (1929–31). When Trevelyan returned to the Board of Education, he had difficulty in convincing the rest of his Party of the feasibility of raising the school leaving age to 15.

In opposition in the pre-war years, the Labour Party still lacked any coherent policy (hence the criticism by Tawney which heads this chapter). The Labour Party policy document of that year (1934) was little more than a list of minor adjustments to Conservative practice — suggestions about fees and special places in grammar schools, rather than a policy on 'secondary education for all'.

This was still the case during the 1939–45 War. When Labour members became part of the coalition government in May 1940, there is no evidence that they played a particularly active part in the discussions of 'education after the war' initiated by the Board of Education's Green Book of that title (June 1941). The Labour Party at that time was not even united on the question of comprehensive schools. And many of those who supported the idea of common schools, perhaps a majority, saw them as a means of improving the process of selection rather than as a way of providing quality secondary education for all children. Like many Conservatives, they wanted a more efficient 'ladder of opportunity' rather than a policy of building 'a broad highway' for all.

The 1945 Labour Party election manifesto *Let Us Face the Future* contained no educational thinking, but simply gave support to the Butler Act. The result was that after the 1945 election, the Labour administration was faced with the task of implementing an Act about which it had no clear policy. The Labour Party, with its first comfortable majority, had a real opportunity to effect change, but the vision of a different kind of education service was still lacking, education was not the highest priority and the Labour government seemed content to put the Education Act into operation in a way which the Conservative Party could find little to argue about.

Not only did the Party lack a coherent policy, but it was still internally divided on the major issue of how to interpret the 1944 Act on the question of secondary school organization: should LEAs be encouraged to have common secondary schools or separation according to ability at 11? The prevailing view seemed to be that separation after a test would be acceptable so long as a doctrine of parity of prestige was adhered to. This was the line consistently taken by the Minister of Education, Ellen Wilkinson, who argued for equality plus diversity. Olive Banks (1955), in her book on this issue, has shown the impossibility of the policy of parity of esteem ever succeeding, given the differences in status attaching to the products of the different kinds of schools. We must, of course, avoid judging the politicians of the 1940s and 1950s in the light of knowledge gained later, but it is still fair to criticize the Labour Party on at least two specific counts: first, they exaggerated the importance of purely administrative changes; and second, they ignored almost completely the importance of the content of education — the curriculum.

Many Labour MPs, including the first Minister, Ellen Wilkinson, and her successor, George Tomlinson, argued that grammar schools were the working class child's alternative to Eton, and even those who unreservedly supported the idea of comprehensive schools, appeared to have given no thought to a curriculum for all children 11 to 16. Some believed that education was simply 'a good thing' and that all should have more of it; others felt that secondary education for all meant a grammar school curriculum for all, without questioning how appropriate the highly academic grammar school curriculum was for the majority of children.

This lack of awareness also resulted in missing the opportunity of integrating independent schools into a national system. By setting up the Fleming Committee on Public Schools, R.A. Butler had avoided the problem: to use his own ambiguous expression, 'the first class carriage had been shunted on to an immense siding' (Butler, 1973, p. 121). There is some reason to believe that, given the post-war optimism and idealism, most independent schools in 1945 would have cooperated with any reasonable scheme to bring the two systems together. But the opportunity was missed by Labour; they accepted the Butler shunt, and the question of private education remains a serious problem to be addressed in the 1990s.

When the Labour Party gave way to a Conservative administration in 1951, it still took several years before any real thought was given by the Labour Party to producing their own education policy. Crosland's *The Future of Socialism* (1956) included a chapter on education (twenty pages out of 529) which was weaker than most of the rest of the book, consisting essentially of a discussion of the relation between education and equality and criticizing the status quo without having a clearly worked out alternative. This deficiency became important a few years later (1964) when Crosland was put in charge of education in the Labour government which came to power after thirteen years of Conservative rule. On this occasion the Labour Party was elected with a programme which included comprehensive secondary education.

Crosland saw that grammar schools and comprehensives could not rationally co-exist in the same catchment area. But he did not appear to appreciate the danger of abolishing grammar schools whilst leaving independent schools to survive unchanged and completely outside the national system, despite his concern earlier to achieve a radical reform of the public schools. Because he could see no immediate way of reforming the public schools in 1965, he pessimistically set up the Public Schools Commission 'to advise on the best way of integrating the public schools with the State system of education', without any hope of a realistic solution (Crosland, 1982, p. 148).

His Circulars to LEAs about the development of comprehensive plans (10/65 and 10/66) were evidence of incomplete thinking on the subject. 10/65 merely commented on six schemes already in existence in some LEAs, without including, or being backed by, any message about the purpose of comprehensive education and the ideals behind it. The approach was bureaucratic rather than political or educational. Crosland himself was frustrated by what he disliked in the grammar schools rather than stimulated by a clear picture of secondary education for all. Hence his angry outburst to Susan Crosland, 'If it's the last thing I do, I am going to destroy every fucking grammar school in England. And Wales. And Northern Ireland' (*ibid*). This has since been used unfairly to show that the Labour Party is willing to destroy good schools.

If Crosland was not an educational thinker himself he did at least listen to the advice of those like the sociologist A.H. Halsey. Crosland believed that socialism must be concerned with greater equality of opportunity in education and in other respects; but every survey since 1944 had confirmed the continuing existence of the powerful link between social class and educational achievement. Halsey was responsible for converting this political perception into remedial policy. Although education does not exist in isolation from other social problems, it is possible to build into the education service 'compensatory' measures. This is in itself a complicated socioeducational problem. Basil Bernstein was later to coin the phrase 'education cannot compensate for society' which should not be interpreted as a criticism of all compensatory programmes, only as an indication that many educational problems are second order problems — that is, caused by poverty, ill-health, inadequate housing and so on. That does not mean, however, that the education service is itself completely powerless to do anything to remedy gross inequalities — hence the policy of 'positive discrimination' in education which in the later 1960s (after the Plowden Report of 1967) took the form of

Education Priority Areas (EPAs) mostly in the inner cities, where additional resources were provided to combat low achievement.

Unfortunately such policies were often criticized from within education (in the USA as well as in the UK), before they were given long enough for adequate evaluation. But aspects of EPA practices survived as policy at LEA level even when the central government changed from Labour to Conservative in 1970. By then the right-wing Black Papers had begun to attack aspects of certain education practices gaining popularity in the Labour years (1964–70), and the focus of educational debate shifted towards criticism of progressive methods and comprehensive reorganization. However, despite the efforts of Halsey and others, the Labour Party still lacked an overall policy on education. There was usually (but not always) a willingness to spend more than the Conservatives, and a growing concern for social justice and equality of opportunity, but little discussion of the purpose of education. Had Crosland remained longer then the influence of Halsey might have been more productive, but Crosland was succeeded as Secretary of State in 1967 by Patrick Gordon Walker (who in Cabinet voted against raising the school leaving age) before handing over to Edward Short in 1968. The dominant influences on education in the 1960s were probably the Newsom Report (1963) and the Plowden Report (1967), but these were not Labour Party documents — both committees were set up by Conservative ministers. Pressure groups such as the Comprehensive Schools Committee (launched in 1965) were advocating genuine comprehensive schools (rather than three schools under one roof), but these existed outside the Labour Party.

Out of office from 1970 to 1974, the Labour Party had a chance to develop policies, but the only change was the more positive attitude towards comprehensive schools: they were now official Labour policy on secondary education and there was a promise to legislate for this by Act of Parliament. But even that was following events rather than pointing the way to a better future and, as has frequently been pointed out, although Margaret Thatcher, as Secretary of State for Education and Science (1970–74) cancelled the Labour Party's Circulars (10/65 and 10/66) about comprehensive planning she was herself responsible for approving more comprehensive plans than any Labour minister. The growth of comprehensive schools was a 'grass roots' trend in LEAs rather than the result of party politics — and the motive was frequently the unpopularity of the demonstrably unfair 11+ examination rather than a commitment to the comprehensive ideal. By the early 1970s it was clear that merely providing comprehensive schools was no panacea for inequality: sociologists such as Julienne Ford (1969) showed that comprehensive schools in themselves did not improve the educational life chances of working class children. In 1973 a Working Party of the Labour Party's National Executive Council Sub-committee on Education and Science, initiated a discussion on core curriculum and its assessment, but it was not greeted with great enthusiasm by the Party.

Back in power under Harold Wilson in 1974, the Labour Party made no further advance in the development of an educational policy either with Reg Prentice as Secretary of State (1974) or Fred Mulley (1975), both of whom were concerned to manage the education service with reducing resources rather than to develop innovatory policies. Wilson had set up a Policy Unit in 1974, but education was never top of the list of priorities. The Policy Unit was influential in education, but at the level of the immediate organization rather than long-term goals: for example, it secured the replacement of the Permanent Secretary, William Pile, by the more dynamic James Hamilton, but did not produce any change in government policy on education.

Callaghan took over as Prime Minister when Wilson resigned in 1976. It is clear from his own autobiography (1987) and from Donoughue's (1987) account that Callaghan had a considerable interest in education, and felt that changes in policy were required. Callaghan's major concerns were 'standards' and 'relevance'; his intervention did not result in a new Labour Party policy, but encouraged civil servants to take up some of the issues which Conservative politicians and their friends had been advocating since the 1969 Black Papers. Chitty (1989) and Jones (1989) have both documented this period in detail and have complained that Callaghan's Ruskin speech (1976) and the Great Debate on education were instrumental in producing a move to the right in education. Both writers also confirm that part of the reason for this reaction was the lack of any real Labour Party policy on education, although in 1973 a Working Party of the National Executive Council's Science and Education Committee had made some forward-looking recommendations, including a core curriculum.

I would put a slightly different emphasis on the events of 1976. Whilst accepting most of the analysis provided by Chitty, for example, I would go further in accepting that drastic action was required in some areas — the William Tyndale scandal was not a completely isolated incident, and many of Callaghan's concerns about primary and secondary education were justified. The education service as a whole was not functioning as effectively as it should have been. Yet it is true that his criticisms played into the hands of the Conservatives. Since there was no coherent Labour Party policy on education, Callaghan's questions and implied criticisms became useful ammunition for the right wing of the Conservative Party who eagerly used the opportunity to promote right-wing ideas about the education service. Callaghan's position was not helped by the fact that his Secretary of State, Shirley Williams, was notoriously indecisive and failed to take action even on the straightforward question of establishing a common examination at 16.

Since 1979, in opposition again, the Labour Party was slow to develop an education policy. They have continued to be satisfied with criticizing Conservative proposals rather than developing their own alternatives. In the election year 1987, the Manifesto *Britain Will Win* was still weak on education. In May 1989, a new policy document *Meet the Challenge Make the Change* was published with stronger references to education, and this was followed by *Children First* which emphasized the importance of education and indicated that the Labour Party would give it a higher priority (and spend more money), but specific policies were difficult to discern. In 1990, the annual conference indicated that education and training should be the top priority for the next Labour government, but there was still a need for a detailed programme with argument and policies rather than slogans. This deficiency was only partly met in 1990/91 with the production of *Aiming High* which talked of raising standards in a variety of sensible ways. But there was a danger that the main thrust of policy would be towards bureaucratic control of the system (with such proposals as the Education Standards Council) rather than an educational ideal. Jack Straw, the Shadow Education Secretary, worked hard to produce a coherent set of policies. To some extent he succeeded, but they are certainly pragmatic rather than visionary, differing only on points of detail from Conservative plans. Perhaps significantly the greatest differences between the policies are, as we shall see in later chapters, on 16–19 education and training and the abolition of 'A' levels.

What is lacking is a principle or set of principles which would clearly differentiate Labour Party policy from that of the Conservatives. Crosland, and before him, Tawney, focused on the ideal of 'equality' — a word which was so ambiguous that it became misleading. (There were endless disputes about whether it meant equality of opportunity, equality of outcome or equality of regard). Equality will no longer serve, but if we examine clearly what has developed as one of the remaining guiding principles of Labour Party policy it is social justice or fairness. This too has problems of definition, but it is an ideal difficult to oppose in principle, although theorists of both wings of the New Right have tried. Essentially what distinguishes Labour Party attitudes to education, and other social issues, is the emphasis on fairness in aiming to provide a worthwhile education *for all*. It could be used more effectively and explicitly as a central ideological core to the Labour Party's education programme.

The purpose of this chapter has been to describe attempts by the Labour Party since 1945 to develop a comprehensive and coherent set of policies in education and to show that far from being dominated by ideology, the Party has suffered from a lack of ideology. I have also indicated my belief that in the 1990s a consensus position of some kind will be desirable. There is a paradox here. Some might suggest that the lack of a powerful ideology on education and the consequent lack of education policies would be an advantage in achieving consensus. Not so. In order to reach a productive, forward-looking consensus, it is necessary for both parties to have clear views on what they think society needs. Only then can political compromises be reached. There is a very important difference between having strong policies but being prepared to adopt a gradualist approach, and being satisfied with doing no more than implementing another

Party's programme with minor amendments. As a preliminary to discussing consensus it will be necessary for each Party to establish, both at the level of ideology and at the level of policy, what it really stands for. In the case of the Labour Party, they will need to be able to translate the metaphor of 'the broad highway' into clearly understood practical programmes.

Chapter 3

Education, Ideology and the Conservative Party from 1944 to 1988

> For nearly forty years from the time of Butler the Party had no real education policy. The Party has always been nervous about its lack of a Conservative educational philosophy. (Robert Dunn, Parliamentary Under-Secretary of State for Education 1983–1986, quoted in Knight, 1990, p. 168)

The 1944 Act, although often referred to as the Butler Act, should not be seen as an example of the expression of Tory policy but as the product of war-time bi-partisan optimism and consensus about a better post-war world. In some respects it was a continuation of the moderate Tory reforms of the 1930s, generally drifting towards education expansion, and providing more secondary opportunities. There were ideological undertones to this drift but many would deny that it constituted policy. Perhaps the major concerns were to avoid spending too much public money on education, to preserve as much of the status quo as possible, and, where change was necessary, to move without undue haste. There were, of course, differences within the Party: a few still regretting the need for direct state participation in education; others seeing the inevitability of an improving education service if England was to remain a free and prosperous industrial society.

The 1944 Act took the development of the system several stages further. Not only were fees abolished, but secondary education was to be provided for *all* — eventually up to the age of 16. Contrasting interpretations of the Act would later provide a specific point of difference from Labour: although the Labour Party was by no means united on the meaning of 'secondary education for all', most Conservatives were sure that it did *not* mean multilateral or comprehensive schools. Official Conservative policy reflected the views of virtually all Conservative MPs, that different kinds of ability should be catered for in different kinds of school, and that the grammar school curriculum should be preserved for able children.

There was no unanimity, however, about the question of the quality of state schools: some Conservatives felt that state schools should necessarily be inferior to what could be purchased privately, but others like David Eccles (Minister of Education 1954–57 and 1959–62) wanted to improve state schools to such an extent that parents would not wish to buy something better (*ibid*, p. 10). Part of his plan (which, he later admitted, never succeeded) was to achieve quality by means of differentiation. When Eccles spoke of quality he clearly meant quality for bright children — especially in the sixth form. He was a meritocrat, believing in quality achieved by a 'ladder of opportunity' for some, not the socialist 'broad highway' for all. Eccles, as a good meritocrat, was particularly concerned to preserve the grammar schools. This policy was already failing in the early 1950s, however, and in 1953 Angus Maude at a Party Conference deplored the attempt to 'comprehensivize the system'. Maude was anxious to preserve denominational schools as well as independent schools.

Yet despite the strength of such views at Party conferences during the thirteen years of Tory rule (1951–64) and in election manifestoes (for example, the 1955 manifesto), the drift away from the tripartite system continued. The reason for this was that local authorities were faced with parents who were dissatisfied with 11+ testing and the quality of secondary modern schools. When LEAs built new schools, these tended to be comprehensive schools, but many Tories still feared that comprehensives could not cater for able pupils.

Another developing feature of Conservative education views in the 1960s was an expression of 'anti-modernism' or 'anti-progressivism' — eventually to be given publicity by Professor Brian Cox and the Black Paper writers.

The end of thirteen years Conservative rule in 1964 was not marked by any unified view on education within the Conservative Party. Blake (1985) described 1963–64 as a time when the Conservatives were demoralized and divided into those who wanted to emphasize tradition (like Angus Maude) and those who saw the need to modernise (like Edward Boyle) (p. 416). Boyle was anti-socialist, believed in selection in education, but not necessarily as early as 11. He thought that the Conservative Party should have an open mind about comprehensive schools. In 1965 the fact that Boyle became Heath's Shadow Spokesman on Education sharpened the problem of developing a coherent education policy within the party. Official Conservative policy followed the Crowther and Newsom Reports' suggestion that it was premature to judge the success or failure of comprehensive schools, and that meanwhile a variety of provision would be desirable. This policy involved defending grammar schools but allowing comprehensive experiments in some areas and, somewhat illogically, having both grammar schools and comprehensive schools in the same areas. It is not surprising therefore that some Conservatives, hoping for a policy further to the right, had complained that 'so few people interested in education seemed to know what our Party policy is' (Longden, quoted by Knight, 1990, p. 30).

The Conservative Party was in a difficult position: sociologists, psychologists and other education experts were continuing to criticize the inefficiency and unfairness of 11+ selection; the majority of parents wanted an alternative to the tripartite system (but did not necessarily have a positive desire for comprehensive schools). It was difficult for anyone as honest as Edward Boyle to pretend that Conservative policy on education was substantially opposed to that of the Labour Party.

The Conservative Research Department's solution to this problem was to elevate Tory liking for 'excellence' and 'parental choice' into public statements of policy. They also began to attack comprehensive schools for being too large. Apart from the unpopularity of the 11+ there was another obstacle to taking policy further to the right. Boyle, who on the education right/ left continuum was not very far from Crosland, was prepared to criticize bad comprehensive plans when they appeared to threaten excellence but not to generalize about the undesirability of comprehensive schools.

There was also a problem of wanting to preserve schools of excellence (grammar schools) whilst acknowledging that selection at 11+ was indefensible. The Conservative answer was to attack, condemning mixed ability grouping as 'the egalitarian threat', deploring the loss of good schools, and, more important in the long run, advocating parental choice and the preservation of independent schools as a means of preventing a state monopoly in education.

Even before the publication of the first Black Paper in 1969, there were signs of a swing to the right: for example, Angus Maude's *Education: Quality and Equality* (1968). Attacks on education policy became part of a general criticism of collectivist policies which restricted freedom, choice and diversity of taste. The Black Papers converted these intellectual anti-egalitarian ideas into a series of populist attacks on 'socialist education', progressive teaching methods, the lack of discipline among the young and an alleged collapse of standards.

This unofficial swing to the right within the Conservative Party was greatly assisted by the violent student demonstrations of 1968 in Paris, USA and also in English universities. The first Black Paper (March 1969) was originally intended by Cox and Dyson to deal exclusively with the problem of universities and their 'falling standards', but they soon found that there were equally strong views concerning 'standards' in primary and secondary schools. The decision to widen the content of the Black Paper in this way proved to be a clever ploy: more voters were interested in schools than in higher education, and it was possible to worry them with horror stories about 'free play' in primary schools, the absence of control in comprehensive schools and so on.

The publication of the first Black Paper was a useful method of generating public debate and encouraging parents and others to be more critical of Labour Party views and policies, but it was no substitute for the formulation of a Conservative education policy. Lord Coleraine (who later founded the Salisbury Group) said that the Party was intellectually confused in the field of education and that the Conservative leadership was 'repeating the prevailing shibboleths without debate of any kind' (Coleraine, 1970, p. 140, quoted by Knight, 1990, p. 61).

A policy was urgently needed. The General Election in 1970 returned Heath as Prime Minister with Margaret Thatcher as Secretary of State for Education and Science. At this time she professed to be a moderate in education but one who believed in 'excellence' (Knight, 1990, p. 62). Her task as Secretary of State was not easy: the drift to many more LEA comprehensive schemes continued, despite her prompt action in cancelling the previous government's Circulars 10/65 and 10/66 which had requested comprehensive plans from LEAs. The Black Papers and other publications, such as Swinton Journal, provided right-wing ammunition, but official Conservative policy on education re-mained 'moderate' — trying to preserve the best whilst encour-aging useful reforms, including many comprehensive schemes. The debate continued to focus on structure until Margaret Thatcher's address to the Association of Education Committees in October 1970 when she made some significant references to the curriculum.

By now the Secretary of State had been briefed by Cox and Dyson and also by the Conservative National Advisory Com-mittee on Education (CNACE) (and especially by Gilbert Longden — see Knight, 1990, p. 68). But it took time to convert these right-wing ideas into official policy, especially when there was still some opposition to 'Black Paper ideology' within the Party. Another right-wing pressure group now entered the fray — the Council for the Preservation of Educational Standards (later re-named National Council for Educational Standards). CPES urged the preservation of traditional standards as the answer to left-wing progressivism. But others were by now wanting much more radical policies, namely, to move the discussion away from the state system to the desirability of *choice* outside state schools, for example, by means of vouchers.

These two ideas — traditional standards and parental choice — were not unconnected: there was an assumption (partly but not entirely correct) that traditional standards were most likely to be found in independent schools. But by mid-1972 the right-wing had still failed to make its mark on official policy, and in Decem-ber 1972 a very conventional DES policy document was published

— *Education: A Framework for Expansion.* However, the appointment of Norman St. John Stevas as a right-wing junior Education Minister, and the disappearance of Edward Boyle from the political scene, made a difference: Margaret Thatcher soon publicly expressed her doubts about any expansion of the system without raising standards, and at the 1973 Party Conference she emphasized the importance of parental choice, including encouraging parents to choose outside the state system. At about the same time, the Labour Party — especially Roy Hattersley — was reaffirming the policy of gradually reducing and eventually abolishing private education; this served to stimulate the Right into organized protection of independent education to guard against 'state monopoly'. St. John Stevas launched a campaign to save direct grant schools, and the Independent Schools Joint Committee (ISJC) was founded in 1974 with Lord Belstead, a Conservative Minister, as its first Chairman. This coincided with the continuing activities of right-wing polemicists (for example, Cox and Boyson, 1977).

Right-wing pressure groups, particularly CNACE, kept up the flow of publications, for example, *Opportunity and Choice in Education* (January 1974), and such documents gradually made an impact. The 1974 Election Manifesto can be seen as a clear shift to the right: standards and parental choice were highlighted, but it was not a dramatic shift, and the Party seemed unwilling to make education a major policy issue. The real change came after the 1974 election. The Heath government was defeated, and in 1975 Margaret Thatcher became Leader of the Party in opposition. Before analyzing these changes it may be important to ask why Margaret Thatcher from 1970 to 1974 made so little impact on education policy. For nearly four years she seemed willing to preside over a DES with policies little different from those of any other government in the 1960s. Why?

There are probably at least three reasons: first, Mrs. Thatcher was busy learning about education and how to be Secretary of State, and for a while trusted the advice of her DES civil servants. Second, it is probable that she did not then know exactly what she wanted in education. Third, she did not wish to risk antagonizing Heath who, as Prime Minister, was likely to play a key role in her political career. (She could not have suspected at that time that she would replace him as leader so soon.)

When Margaret Thatcher became Leader of the Party in 1975, however, the prospects for a change in policy were quite different; moreover the Party now had the benefit of advice from a newly established 'Think Tank', the Centre for Policy Studies (CPS) — founded by Sir Keith Joseph in 1974. One of the first pieces of advice was about *vouchers* as a means of achieving freedom and choice in education. Although vouchers repeatedly failed to be adopted as Party policy, they became an important symbol of market ideas in education which were eventually so important. But vouchers divided even the right-wing of the Conservative Party: Brian Cox, Stevas, Greenway and Ollerenshaw were at that time all opposed to vouchers.

In 1975 the right-wingers were presented with a gift in the form of the William Tyndale scandal. William Tyndale was a primary school in Islington where parents had complained about the introduction of radical changes in teaching — children were allowed a good deal of choice, including whether or not to learn to read. The report of the official inquiry (The Auld Report, 1976), appeared to be very critical of the lack of control over the Head and the left-wing teachers who had created the situation. Many of the evils that right-wing scaremongers had predicted could be found at William Tyndale!

In the autumn of 1975 Margaret Thatcher set up an education policy review which continued to meet and make recommendations for the next three years under the chairmanship of Norman St. John Stevas, the opposition spokesman on education 1974–78. It is also significant that during this period the right-wing Stuart Sexton was officially Education Advisor to the Opposition (1975–79). But a three-year period for the review turned out to be too long: in 1976, before the Conservatives managed to publish *The Right Approach*, the Prime Minister, James Callaghan, stole the Conservative thunder by making a speech on education himself, and by showing concern for some of the same education issues — standards, the curriculum, teaching quality and so on.

In November 1976, the Conservative policy-making machine took a lurch to the right when Rhodes Boyson was appointed as Stevas's deputy spokesman on education. He was ideologically further to the right than Stevas: they agreed on many aspects of policy but disagreed about vouchers and the publication of school examination reports in the form of league tables (Sexton agreed with Boyson on both issues). In January 1977, Stevas launched 'Standards 77' (a campaign to raise standards in schools) which involved giving higher priority to religious and moral education and even supported the need for political education.

Knight (1990), however, suggests that even this aggressive Stevas line was still too moderate for Boyson and the right-wing pressure groups, especially on such 'choice' issues as the publication of examination results. But although the Party was moving steadily to the right in education, when Stevas became Shadow Leader of the House, Boyson did not replace him as Education Spokesman; instead, Mark Carlisle, a confused moderate on education, took over and eventually became Secretary of State for Education and Science after the 1979 election. Stuart Sexton continued as education advisor.

Carlisle's first major problem, as Secretary of State, was not policy but money: how to enable the education service to survive the 7 per cent cuts in expenditure demanded by the monetarists. There was, apparently, little Cabinet discussion of education policy at this time. Carlisle resisted pressures to adopt vouchers, but he did, despite the cuts, introduce, in the 1980 Act, the Assisted Places Scheme promised in the Election Manifesto. The Assisted Places Scheme subsidized places in independent schools for 'able' pupils whose parents could not afford to pay full fees (see Edwards *et al*, 1989). It was a policy which provided the clearest example of ideological differences between the Labour Party and the Conservative Party from 1980 onwards.

Carlisle was soon replaced by the considerably less moderate Sir Keith Joseph. Sexton continued as education advisor. Joseph faced an enormous personal problem of reconciling the notion of 'free market, minimum (but strong) state' with the immediate needs of the education service. Knight (1990) has secured from Sir Keith Joseph a summary of his own education policy thinking which throws some light on his dilemma:

Like Angus Maude, I was a One Nation group member in 1956. We believed levelling in schools had to stop and that excellence (discrimination) had to return. Our key perception was differentiation. We equated the stretching of children, at all levels of ability, with caring. Our aim was to achieve rigour in the school curriculum. Later, I was much influenced by Maude's views in *The Common Problem*, and the Black Papers. The Black Papers responded to a strong national perception, that there was a vast gap between what people received and what people needed in education. Because of the fall in the birth rate and school rolls, I decided, when I took office in 1981, to go for quality not quantity. (p. 152)

An essential difference about Joseph's policies was that he rejected the status quo and sought radical change. He was known to be an enthusiast for the operations of the market, even in education, and admired the writings of Hayek and Friedman who both had objections to the principle of state controlled education.

Joseph was officially committed to making the comprehensive system work more efficiently, but he was also known to be in favour of various kinds of selection, including the Assisted Places Scheme, which would inevitably undermine comprehensive structures in LEAs. The most obvious way of moving education further into the market would have been the introduction of a voucher system. This had long been advocated by many right-wingers; now, vocal individuals such as Rhodes Boyson, had reason to expect that they had a Secretary of State willing to introduce such a scheme. They were disappointed: the many opponents of vouchers in the Party and in the DES were able to show how much 'disruption' would be involved at LEA level; more importantly, it could be demonstrated that the financial costs of vouchers would be enormous. One of the arguments used in support of vouchers was that they would enable parents to escape from such intolerable schools as William Tyndale. But, as we shall see, there were other ways of achieving that objective. Vouchers were not included in the 1983 Election Manifesto; and at the 1983 Party Conference Joseph announced that the idea of vouchers in education was dead. He was, of course, wrong.

Another of Joseph's concerns was teacher training. The 1983 Manifesto explicitly mentioned Conservative dissatisfaction with the selection and training of teachers and made reference to the DES White Paper *Teaching Quality* (1983b). The Manifesto also stated that teachers would be required to keep adequate records of pupils' progress. But neither of these were the major policies that those on the right of the Party had been expecting.

Perhaps the greatest shift in education policy, sometimes referred to as the 'new vocationalism', was initiated not by the DES but by the Department of Employment/Manpower Services Commission (MSC) in the form of the Technical and Vocational Education Initiative (TVEI). In fairness to Joseph, however, it has to be said that for some time he had been concerned about the national curriculum, especially the needs of the least able 40 per cent of pupils. In October 1983 he had issued a draft Circular reminding LEAs of their curricular responsibilities. He followed this up in Sheffield at the January 1984 North of England Conference on Education, outlining major policy changes. He redefined the 5–16 curriculum in terms of 'breadth, relevance, differentiation and balance'; raising standards of achievement (so that between 80 and 90 per cent of pupils would be expected to achieve what was then the 'average'); and shifting the examination and assessment system away from norm-referencing to criterion-referencing so that real changes could be measured.

The 'new vocationalism' has been seen by many critics to be the major shift in education policy. Some have identified David Young as the main thinker behind this new emphasis, especially the concern that employers should have much greater say about the curriculum and other educational matters. Such a shift in educational purpose did not, however, meet with wholehearted approval within the Party. Knight shows that Roger Scruton, for example, thought that Joseph was completely mistaken to turn in this 'consumerist-technicist' direction (p. 171). For similar reasons, Enoch Powell later (December 1984) referred to the Thatcher state as 'inhuman and barbarous'. But the new Joseph line prevailed at the 1984 Party Conference and was soon transformed from Party policy into a DES publication *Better Schools* (1985).

The new Conservative tough policy on education, criticizing schools, teachers and teacher trainers, was given additional support by the disastrous teachers' pay dispute involving the kind of industrial action which parents found not only inconvenient but morally offensive. The Conservatives had increasingly adopted a moral stance on education which appeared to be finding some favour with the public, despite the popular suspicion that more money was needed to improve the education service. A little ammunition for the right-wing, anti-teacher, 'low standards' faction had been provided in 1983 by Sig Prais and K. Wagner of the National Institute of Economic and Social Research (NIESR) who compared mathematics standards in English schools and in West Germany. Prais and Wagner (*Schooling Standards in Britain and Germany*, NIESR, 1983) reworked data from the 1964 International Educational Achievement Study and claimed to demonstrate that German pupils in the bottom half of the ability range obtained levels of performance comparable with the average for the whole ability range in England. Stuart Maclure (1989) was probably correct in his suggestion that this publication was important because it moved the argument away from comparisons over time to comparisons of our schools now with those of other countries.

Gradually, however, some of the contradictions within the Conservative policies proved too much for Keith Joseph — especially the conflict between the needs of a state system and the desirability of choice. In May 1986 he resigned as Secretary of State, saying, in a letter to the Prime Minister that 'A fresh voice is needed at the DES to carry forward and develop our policies'. Maclure suggests (1989) that 'The Joseph prescription was, essentially, the Callaghan consensus in action' (p. 167). But this was obscured by Joseph's unpopularity with teachers and LEAs. By dwelling on the shortcomings of the system and 'ineffective teachers' with low expectations of their pupils (especially the bottom 40 per cent), he helped to prepare public opinion for radical change. Despite (or perhaps because of) the strength of his convictions on education, Joseph left education policy in a state of confusion. Finding a suitable person to fill the role of Secretary of State was a crucial decision for Margaret Thatcher. She chose Kenneth Baker, who had not hitherto been thought of as a right-winger on educational matters. His agenda for education had already been very largely set: partly by a Cabinet Committee on Education and partly by the reactionary economist, Professor Brian Griffiths, Head of the Prime Minister's Policy Unit.

Tory education policy 1979–1988 was inevitably something of an anomaly. Gamble (1990) has argued that Thatcherism has two major planks (the free economy and the strong state) together with a moral concern for the family. This ideology was used to defeat trade unions, encourage privatization, reduce public expenditure and abolish exchange controls. But education, even more than health, presented difficulties. We have seen that vouchers, the main hope for those wishing to introduce the free market into education, had to be abandoned before the 1983 election, and was not to be revived until 1990. Instead, Kenneth Baker put together a mixture of measures in the Education Reform Act 1988 which represented a desire to encourage more parental choice whilst leaving the state system relatively intact. Thus the strong state must, as second best policy, control the education system more rigorously — hence the centralized national curriculum and its assessment, tighter regulations for teacher training, and more financial control over higher education.

By 1988 it was no longer possible to classify Conservative politicians as modernizers or traditionalists in their educational thinking, as Boyle and Maude had been described earlier (Blake, 1985); the New Right discussions had complicated the picture and prevented the development of a single ideology on education. Neo-liberals like Sexton had quite different views from Scruton and others who wanted a renewed stress on traditional conservative values. Both groups agreed on opposing certain 'leftish' ideas such as comprehensive schools, but they disagreed on much more. Only occasionally did these disputes become public (for example, when Peregrine Worsthorne (in *Too Much Freedom*, 1978) said that the state should 'reassert its authority, and it is useless to imagine that this will be helped by some libertarian mish-mash drawn from the writings of Adam Smith, John Stuart Mill and the warmed-up milk of nineteenth century liberalism'). But that was a rare lapse a long time ago. Generally Conservatives keep much quieter about their ideological disputes than those in the Labour Party. Nevertheless, the underlying differences (see appendix below) do present problems for a reforming Secretary of State, and this was clearly the case in 1988, as we shall see in chapter 4.

Appendix

Right-Wing Pressure Groups and Some of Their Publications

ASI (Adam Smith Institute): A free market publishing group established in 1977. Hayek, Madsen Pirie, Fallon, 'The Omega Project'.

BPG (Black Paper Group): 1969: Brian Cox — links with CQS.

CPG (Conservative Philosophy Group): Roger Scruton active member; in 1970s Thatcher, Boyson, Worsthorne, Flew.

CPS (Centre for Policy Studies): Anti-statist, free market, established by Sir Keith Joseph in 1974; Sherman.

CQS (Critical Quarterly Society): Brian Cox, Dyson (see BPG).

CRE (Campaign for Real Education): Deuchar (1989).

ERC (Education Research Centre): Scruton, Ellis-Jones and O'Keeffe (1985).

FEVER (Friends of the Education Voucher Experiment in Representative Regions): founded 1974; Seldon (1986).

HG (Hillgate Group): Scruton, Caroline Cox, Marks, Norcross; often published by Claridge Press.

IEA (Institute of Economic Affairs): 1955; began publishing 1957; Lord Harris; Sexton heads Education Unit.

NTB (No Turning Back Group): 1985: right wing Conservative MPs including Fallon, Howarth, Brown *et al* (1986).

SAU (Social Affairs Unit): 1980: Director Digby Anderson, Advisory Council includes O'Keeffe.

SG (Salisbury Group): Links with CPG but not officially with Conservative Party. Scruton editor of *Salisbury Review*.

Selected Publications on Education Since 1969 (First Black Paper)

ANDERSON, D. *et al* (1981) *The Pied Pipers of Education*. SAU.

ASI (1985) *The Omega File*, ASI.

BOYSON, R. (Ed.) (1970) *Right Turn*, Churchill Press.

BOYSON, R. (Ed.) (1972) *Education: Threatened Standards*, Churchill Press.

BOYSON, R. (1975) *The Crisis in Education*, Woburn Press.

BROWN, M., CHOPE, C., FALLON, M., FORTH, E., FORSYTH, M., HAMILTON, N., HOWARTH, A., JONES, R., LEIGH, E., LILLEY,

P., PORTILLO, M. and TWINN, I. (1986) *Save Our Schools*, Conservative Political Centre.

COX, C., *et al* (1975) *Rape of Reason: The Corruption of the Polytechnic of North London*, Churchill Press.

COX, C. and MARKS, J. (1988) *The Insolence of Office-Education and the Civil Servants*, Claridge Press.

COX, C.B. and DYSON, A. (1969) *Fight for Education: A Black Paper*, CQS.

DENNISON, S.R. (1984) *Choice in Education*, IEA.

DEUCHAR, S. (Ed.) (1989) *What is Wrong With Our Schools?*, CRE.

FLEW, A. (1987) *Power to the Parents: Reversing Educational Decline*, Sherwood Press.

HILLGATE GROUP (1987) *The Reform of British Education*, Claridge Press.

HILLGATE GROUP (1989) *Learning to Teach*, Claridge Press.

JOSEPH, K. (1976) *Stranded in the Middle Ground*, CPS.

JOSEPH, K. and SUMPTION, J. (1979) *Equality*, John Murray.

LAWLOR, S. (1989) 'Correct core', CPS.

LETWIN, O. (1988) *Privatising the World*, Cassell.

LETWIN, O. (1989) 'Grounding comes first', CPS.

MARKS, J. (1984) *Peace Studies in our Schools: Propaganda for Defencelessness*, Women and Families for Defence.

MAYNARD, A. (1975) *Experiment with Choice in Education*, IEA.

NAYLOR, F. (1987) *Alarm over A-Level*, CPS.

NAYLOR, F. and MARKS, J. (1985) *Comprehensives: Counting the Cost*, CPS.

NORCROSS, L. and BROWN, P. (1989) *GCSE*, IEA.

O'HEAR, A. (1988) *Who Teaches the Teachers?*, SAU.

O'KEEFFE, D. (Ed.) (1986) *The Wayward Curriculum*, SAU.

O'KEEFFE, D. (1990) *The Wayward Elite: A Critique of British Teacher-Education*, ASI.

SCRUTON, R. (1981) *The Politics of Culture and Other Essays*, Carcanet.

SCRUTON, R. (1984) 'Why teach philosophy to children who can't add up?', *Daily Mail*, 3 February.

SCRUTON, R. *et al* (1985) *Education and Indoctrination*, ERC Sherwood Press.

SELDON, A. (1986) *The Riddle of the Voucher*, IEA.

SEXTON, S. (1987) *Our Schools — A Radical Policy*, IEA.

SEXTON, S. (Ed.) (1988) *GCSE A Critical Analysis*, IEA.

Chapter 4

The Growth of Ideological Conflicts: The Education Reform Act (1988)

Our education system has operated over the past forty years on the basis of the framework laid down by Rab Butler's 1944 Act, which in turn built on the Balfour Act of 1902. We need to inject a new vitality into that system. It has become producer-dominated. It has not proved sensitive to the demands for change that have become ever more urgent over the past ten years. This Bill will create a new framework, which will raise standards, extend choice and produce a better educated Britain. (Kenneth Baker, in the debate on the Second Reading of the Bill, 1 December 1987)

We have seen from the later sections of chapters 2 and 3, and especially from the events of 1976–77, that the desire for education reform was not confined to the Right. There were legitimate complaints about organization, curriculum planning and teaching methods which needed to be addressed. The approach to education reform might have continued in the tradition of consensus operating since 1944. But it was not to be. The ERA (1988) was presented explicitly as a set of radical right-wing propositions, some of them clearly derived from the publications of various right-wing think tanks (Haviland, 1988). Whereas the Butler Act was deliberately bipartisan and consensus-seeking, the ERA (1988) was aggressively ideological and political. Consequently it took more than 360 hours of Parliamentary time before the Reform Bill became the 1988 Act. It gave the Secretary of State for Education and Science 415 new powers, and provoked much opposition, not least because it shifted power away from LEAs to the central authority, contrary to the established tradition of avoiding too much centralized control.

We have to ask why the Act took that particular form, and why it appeared in 1988 (after nine years of government), as well as why it provoked so much criticism and hostility inside and outside Parliament.

Some have identified 'choice' as the key factor in the 1988 legislation. Stewart Ranson (1990), for example, analyzes three (overlapping) stages in the formulation of that consumerist doctrine: stage 1: (1969–77) when Black Paper writers and others attacked the quality of the education system and stressed the need to strengthen the 'voice of parents'; stage 2: (1974–84) the development of the idea of a 'parents' charter' and legislation (the 1980 Education Act) which provided for more information for parents, more choice of school, and strengthened the representation of parents on governing bodies; stage 3: (1984–88) greatly enhancing powers for parents, culminating in the ERA (1988).

In the attack on 'standards', child-centred teaching methods were at first blamed, but later the criticisms included aspects of 'new curriculum' such as peace studies, anti-racism and other aspects of egalitarian social engineering. The cause of these mistaken goals, it was suggested, was the fact that education had become dominated by producers rather than consumers. The remedy would be to give more power to parents who would, by exercising choice, redress the balance. But just in case, a national curriculum was set up which would enforce standards by very different — planned — measures.

It should not, of course, be forgotten that there was a good deal of legislation on education between 1979 and 1988 (see the appendix to this chapter). The ERA should be seen as a continuation of the trend towards conflict beginning in 1979 rather than a bolt from the blue in 1988. The conflict arose out of the steady erosion of planning and its replacement by the ideology of 'choice'. In 1979 the Education Act repealed the requirement that LEAs should plan for comprehensive reorganization. The 1980 Education Act is something of a ragbag. Perhaps the most important innovation was the Assisted Places Scheme, giving parents of 'able' children an opportunity to have a subsidized place at an independent school (indicating to the public that LEA provision was not really good enough for bright children); the 1980 Act also gave parents the right to choose a school, but, at this stage, the LEA could refuse on grounds of efficiency (and parents had a right of appeal); parents were also given rights of representation on governing bodies; they also had to be provided with information on criteria for admission, examination results and curriculum; the right of LEAs to refuse places for pupils outside their area was restricted.

The 1981 Education Act was concerned with LEA responsibilities for children with special educational needs. The 1984 Education (Grants and Awards) Act permitted the government to allocate money to LEAs for specific purposes, reducing LEA control over the block grant.

In 1986 there were two Education Acts: one required maintained schools to have a governing body and set a formula for representation. The Act also defined the duties of governing bodies. The other Education Act in 1986 was concerned with a specific GRIST scheme for the in-service training of teachers — a further example of central direction of funding which limited LEA discretion.

The 1987 Teachers' Pay and Conditions Act abolished the negotiating procedures set up in 1965. The 1988 Local Government Act included a clause which prevented local authorities from promoting 'teaching in any maintained school of the acceptability of homosexuality as a pretended family relationship'. (This was later superseded by the 1988 Act but is interesting as an example of the growth of central control.) All of this legislation between 1979 and 1988 can be seen as a drift away from local planning to the consumerist position of enhancing parents' choice.

Parental choice was still one major driving force behind ERA, but there was another — the need for 'accountability' — value for money. At this point we can detect a dispute between the neo-liberal privatizers, who wanted to rely on market choice to solve the problem, and the neo-Conservative minimalists who wanted to supplement market forces by applying another kind of quality control — the National Curriculum and its assessment. Privatizers like Sexton (1988) continued to object to a National

Curriculum because it was both unnecessary and intrusive, whereas Baker and others saw the National Curriculum as a method of central control and accountability, as well as a means of providing choice-information for parents.

Thus there were some criticisms of ERA from the right as well as from the left and centre, although major concessions had been made to the New Right in the drafting of the Bill. It is a mistake to look for ideological coherence in the Act as a whole. It is a messy set of compromises between neo-liberal and neo-conservative policies.

I will not attempt to describe the Act in detail (a task already admirably executed by Maclure, 1989), but will focus on the ideological significance of the most important aspects of the Act.

✗ The National Curriculum (Sections 1–25)

Introducing a National Curriculum could have been the means of achieving a new consensus, but the opportunity was missed. By the mid-1980s there was a good deal of support inside and outside the teaching profession for the principle of a National Curriculum. This was partly the result of HMI activity since the early 1970s, developing and quietly publicizing their version of an 'entitlement curriculum' based on 'areas of experience' rather than a list of subjects. Low profile implementation of that kind of core curriculum in a small number of LEA schools had resulted in cautious optimism (DES, 1977, 1981 and 1987) about the usefulness of the model. The HMI Red Books 1, 2 and 3 might have become the basis of a set of national guidelines agreed with the teaching profession. But when the curriculum sections of the Education Reform Bill were written, HMI expertise and experience were ignored, and a National Curriculum was produced which was based simply on the list of subjects that education ministers and their civil servants had presumably studied at school. The only innovations were that technology was included as one of the ten compulsory foundation subjects, and three subjects (English, maths and science) were given priority as the core. There was little difference between the National Curriculum 1988 and the curriculum stipulated in the 1904 Secondary Regulations.

This unimaginative and atheoretical approach was much criticized at the time (Haviland, 1988) and was later to give rise to considerable problems of local curriculum design: important subject matter such as health education, economic under-standing and moral education had to be squeezed in as 'cross-curricular' themes.

The motives for a National Curriculum were a contradictory mixture of bureaucratic centralism and the privatizers' desire to introduce market mechanisms into state schools. There had been a trend since 1977 to shift power — including curriculum control — to the centre, and a compulsory core curriculum was a logical conclusion of that. But a major intention of the Act was to extend market forces by means of parental choice. To choose between schools, parents would need evidence — the information provided by National Curriculum assessment which could be converted into 'league tables' of schools. High achieving schools would become more popular, and low achieving schools would eventually close.

In the context of these contradictory requirements, those concerned with devising a scheme of assessment for the National Curriculum were given an almost impossible task: to produce a system which would be educationally respectable, administratively manageable, and also provide the 'political' data required for rank ordering schools — and all in about five months! The Task Group for Assessment and Testing (TGAT) chaired by Professor Paul Black, nevertheless produced a report which was welcomed by many educationists. The TGAT assessment model was perhaps the most forward-looking aspect of the National Curriculum and could have been the basis of serious reforms. However, partly because the government rushed ahead impatiently and partly because they neglected to win over the teachers who would have to administer the tests, the assessment materials produced, especially at Key Stage 1, were greatly criticized for a number of reasons (see chapters 5 and 7) and especially for taking up too much time and interfering with normal teaching and learning.

Meanwhile, right-wing attacks on the National Curriculum continued. In 1987 the Institute for Economic Affairs (IEA), unimpressed by the fact that National Curriculum assessment could be used to provide useful market information, condemned the idea of a National Curriculum:

> The most effective National Curriculum is that set by the market, by the consumers of the education service. This will be far more responsive to children's needs and society's demands than any centrally imposed curriculum, no matter how well meant. Attempts by government and by Parliament to impose a curriculum, no matter how 'generally agreed' they think it to be, are a poor second best in terms of quality, flexibility and responsiveness to needs than allowing the market to decide and setting the system free to respond to the overwhelming demand for higher standards. The government must trust market forces rather than some committee of the great and good. (IEA, 1987, quoted by Haviland, 1988, p. 28)

During the House of Lords debate on the Act, Keith Joseph, the previous Secretary of State for Education, (now Lord Joseph), opposed the detailed nature of the National Curriculum. After the Act was passed, Stuart Sexton and others continued to criticize the idea of a National Curriculum, which Sexton insisted on referring to as the 'nationalized curriculum'.

Open Enrolment (Sections 26–32)

A purer example of right-wing ideology almost guaranteed to generate conflict was the provisions relating to 'open enrolment' to county and voluntary schools. This was the result of strong pressure from the privatizers. The ideological objective was to facilitate more parental power by requiring all schools to accept pupils up to their maximum capacity rather than up to a target set by an LEA plan. This was a blatantly consumerist ploy subordinating LEA regard for overall efficiency and economy to parental choice. As had been promised in the 1987 Conservative Election Manifesto, schools were to be compelled 'to respond to the views of parents' — so long as there was space. It was sometimes also claimed by enthusiasts for this kind of choice that whilst good schools would expand, bad schools would eventually close — the market would triumph. An additional advantage claimed was that not only would more attention be paid to the consumers, but that this kind of choice reduced producer dominance.

This bit of enforced competition was received with a good deal of critical scepticism. There were many dangers in giving market forces priority over LEA and school planning. For example, schools which were, or were thought to be, inferior, would lose pupils (and funding) and thereby probably become even more inferior — a perfect recipe for producing sink schools. Many, like the Catholic Bishops, claimed that a superior policy would have been to take measures to ensure that all schools reached adequate standards, rather than run the risk of improving quality for some but reducing standards for others.

A more fundamental criticism was addressed to the idea of competition itself. Schools have always competed in some ways, but on educational matters they have tended to cooperate as part of a system. Many critics of ERA argued that unbridled competition for pupils bearing cash grants would do more harm than good. This criticism was sometimes associated with the view that technical difficulties of presenting examination and assessment results fairly would not enable parents to make rational choices. The TGAT Report had warned against trying to adjust tests scores for environmental factors: raw scores were recommended for use in published results. But raw scores can be very misleading unless account is taken of the starting point of the pupils — i.e., it is the 'value-added' element of the schools' performance which indicates efficiency, not the raw scores (many high scoring schools in middle class areas can be shown to be under-achieving) (see Goldstein, 1987). This problem has remained unresolved.

Local Management of Schools (LMS)
(Sections 33–51)

Long before the Act a number of LEAs had tried out various schemes of local financial management (LFM), some of them very successful. Delegating budgets to schools was not a contentious issue. It was regarded as desirable so long as a fair formula could be found. But the Act went further in two ways: by requiring all LEAs to delegate various staff management responsibilities to schools; and by making these requirements compulsory (for all secondary schools and for all primary schools with more than 200 pupils). Many argued strongly against the operation of the particular scheme which emerged from ERA. In particular, they disliked the specification of 'formula funding' — i.e., LEAs were required to pass on funds to schools on a per capita basis. LEAs were allowed to propose weighting (for example, for children with special needs), but their discretion to plan regionally was severely limited. Another problem of the formula was that staffing costs were based on 'average salaries' so that schools with experienced and more expensive staff were allocated insufficient funds to pay them. This had the strange result of transforming an attempt to attain higher standards into a process for making good, experienced teachers redundant.

The governing bodies of schools became responsible not only for managing the budget, but also for a number of matters relating to the appointment and management of staff. The power of the LEA to lay down an 'establishment' for each school was also removed by the Act.

It was also observed that there was a dangerous link between LMS and open enrolment: by making the budget of a school automatically dependent on the number of pupils, the government was encouraging the schools to compete for students. Many headteachers who liked the idea of delegated financial management, did not approve of the market competition forced on them. Stuart Maclure (1989) and others have pointed out that the combination of open enrolment and per capita funding in effect produced the same result as the voucher systems which had been urged on successive Secretaries of State by Stuart Sexton and other privatizers. Vouchers had been declared a dead issue by Keith Joseph in 1983; but by 1988 they were unnecessary for the school system — market forces could be encouraged by the simple mechanism of attaching a price to every pupil and encouraging schools to compete for the pupils.

Grant Maintained Schools (GMS) (Sections 52–104)

The idea of a category of schools free from LEA control but receiving government funding had been under discussion for some years. Both Keith Joseph and Kenneth Baker had referred to the possibility of reviving something like the direct grant school, and in 1985 and 1986 the 'No Turning Back' group proposed a scheme for parents to start their own school and to receive direct funding from the DES as well as seeking private funds wherever possible (Brown *et al*, 1985). Such schools would have just as much autonomy as independent schools.

Similarly, at about the same time, the Hillgate Group (1986) were working on a proposal that 'ownership' of state schools should be transferred to trusts. In response to these right-wing pressure groups, a new category of schools was created by allowing schools to 'opt out' of LEA control and have a direct financial relationship with the DES. All secondary schools were able to apply for grant maintained status, but primary schools had to have 300 or more pupils to be eligible. In keeping with consumerist concern for parental choice, the decision to apply for grant maintained status rests with parents — by secret postal ballot.

This provision, more than any other aspect of ERA, aroused the hostility of LEAs and others (Haviland, 1988). The main objection is an obvious one: how can an LEA make plans for the region as a whole if an unknown number of schools are allowed to opt out, taking a percentage of LEA finance with them? If there were very few grant maintained schools in existence then LEAs could, presumably, carry on with minor adjustments, but it soon became clear that the government and some civil servants regarded GMS as a logical extension of LMS — one further step away from LEA control on the road to complete independence. There appeared to be a difference of opinion between those Conservative politicians who regarded the *threat* of GMS as producing healthy competition and keeping a few left-wing LEAs in order, and those closer to the privatizer position who saw LMS and GMS as the way to undermine all LEAs and then to abolish them. Many Conservative-controlled LEAs were very hostile to the GMS idea. Churches also opposed the proposals for GMS — not least because the Act enabled parents to seek grant maintained status even if it conflicted with the policy declared by the Trustees. This is exactly what did happen with two Roman Catholic schools in the London area. Apart from a fear of schools 'changing character', the Church of England and Roman Catholic hierarchies disliked the GMS provision for reasons similar to those of the LEAs — it put their overall planning at risk.

Jack Straw, the Labour Party Education Spokesman in 1987, voiced the opinion not only of his Party but also of a much wider group who felt that a planned service was preferable to the chancy operations of the market:

> No single issue caused more trouble for the Conservatives during the 1987 General Election than their manifesto proposal to allow individual schools to 'opt-out' of local authority control. Even the *Sunday Times*, whose loyalty to the Conservatives was never in doubt, was forced to publish a major feature under the headline, 'Schools: Tory Plan That Didn't Add Up'. (Haviland, 1988, p. 103)

City Technology Colleges (CTCs) (Section 105)

The promotion of CTCs, which did not require new legislation, pre-dated discussion of the 1988 Act. CTCs are independent schools receiving special support (where necessary) from the DES. The intention was to provide urban inner city areas with a school which would be a centre of excellence, preferably paid for by private funds.

Progress has been much slower than expected, partly because it has not always been easy to find 'benefactors'. This drew from Jack Straw the complaint that 'the government's original intention of setting up private schools with private money has now changed to setting up private schools with public money' (quoted in Bash and Coulby, 1989, p. 42).

The few CTCs that have been established serve as a means of blurring the distinction between state and private schools; CTCs are closer to full independent status than GM schools, but in reality fall short of real autonomy. Although not required to follow the national curriculum in detail, they are to have regard for its principles. Like GM schools, they considerably inhibit the LEAs' ability to plan a whole system. LEAs have been hostile to CTCs because large sums of money have been siphoned off to subsidize a small number of privileged schools.

Higher and Further Education (Sections 120–138)

Higher education had been under attack for some years. The provisions of the ERA went much further than most earlier recommendations for reform. The University Grants Committee (UGC), consisting largely, but not entirely, of university professors was replaced by the Universities Funding Council (UFC) which had a much larger number of lay members from industry and commerce. The clear intention was to control expenditure and policy rather than simply sharing out funds between the universities in the UGC style. Universities could no longer expect to receive public funds without much tighter controls over how it was to be spent.

Polytechnics and large colleges of higher education were removed from LEA control, becoming part of a national system of higher education, financed by the new Polytechnics and Colleges Funding Council (PCFC) — a similar mix of academic and business experience to the new UFC.

The mechanism for funding by UFC and PCFC was intended to be by contract based on formulae. Higher education institutions would be contracted to run courses and be paid on a per capita basis. They would also be contracted to do research. This was a monumental change in the relation between the government and higher education (especially the universities), and was condemned by Maurice Kogan (1989) as 'managerialism'. It was not unexpected. For years some Vice-Chancellors and higher education experts had warned of the increasing dependence on the state. Stuart Maclure (1989) summed it up in this way:

It is difficult to exaggerate the magnitude of the change in the management of British HE implicit in these sections of the Act. One set of long-standing conventions has been swept away. The foundations have shifted. The idea of universities as independent centres of learning and research, capable of standing out against government and society, and offering critical judgements of varying objectivity, informed by learning and protected by the autonomy of historic institutions, is discarded. Instead universities are made the servants of the State and its priorities. In the context of the late twentieth century they, like the rest of the education system, are to be used in the attempt to create a nation of enterprise and to discredit the 'dependency culture' associated with the forty years after World War II. (p. 93)

In the House of Lords attempts were made to limit the powers of UFC because it was feared that a Council acting under the instruction of a Secretary of State would adopt the kind of contract system contained in the earlier White Paper. When the Bill went back to the Commons, however, the Secretary of State agreed to a modification of wording but not of substance. The intention to have a contractual relationship with the Secretary of State in a dominant position remained. This provides us with another interesting example of a contradiction between two policies: the desire for central control of HE in the context of an incompatible desire to introduce market forces. Maclure (1989) spotted the contradiction but preferred to talk in terms of 'irony':

As soon as the Act became law ministers began to recognize the irony of an administration which favoured market-based decision-making, adopting a *dirigiste* attitude towards higher education. From the autumn of 1988, the emphasis changed and the funding councils were encouraged to look for ways of distributing monies which would reward institutional entrepreneurship, and decentralized decisions'. (p. 95)

Similar changes in funding were brought in for polytechnics and colleges. The PCFC replaced the National Advisory Body (NAB), and LEAs lost all control over HE. At first colleges of FE remained within LEA planning, but in 1990 it was proposed by the Secretary of State that these should also be taken away from LEAs, and in 1991 the proposal was extended to include sixth-form colleges.

A good deal of publicity was given to the much less important issue of loss of 'tenure' for academic staff. There was much talk about the danger of loss of freedom, but these dangers were much less significant than the changes of funding already discussed.

Locally Funded FE and HE (Sections 139–155)

Having taken the control of polytechnics and larger colleges of higher education away from the LEAs, the aim of the Secretary of State in these sections was to apply to FE colleges principles of financial delegation which were broadly similar to those pertaining to the Local Management of Schools. All colleges with 200 or more full-time students had to have their 'budget share' delegated from the LEA to the governing body. (This arrangement was short-lived because it was superseded by the 1990–91 decision to remove all FE colleges from LEA control.)

Inner London (Sections 162–196)

In its 1987 Election Manifesto, the Conservative Party had promised to allow inner London boroughs to opt out of ILEA control if they wished to. This would have been a means of allowing Conservative-controlled boroughs such as Wandsworth and Westminster to free themselves from the policies of the ILEA. After the Election, however, it became clear that the ILEA would have had considerable difficulty in making any reasonable plans in the face of such uncertainty, and Dr. Williams Stubbs (the ILEA Education Officer) advised his Education Committee that orderly administration could not be sustained (Stubbs, 1988). The revised proposal, put into the amended Bill and passing into law despite considerable opposition in both Houses, was the complete abolition of the ILEA. For many years the Conservatives had accused the ILEA of extravagance and inefficiency (high spending with poor examination results) due to the size and excessively bureaucratic structures in the Authority. In addition, the ILEA had constantly opposed Conservative education policies, attempted to subvert them, and was known for its anti-sexist and anti-racist policies. The evidence about extravagance and standards was not in line with Conservative accusations. The HMI Report on the ILEA in 1987 was reasonably balanced between criticism and support, and acknowledged the unique difficulties of an inner city authority catering for 160 different languages. Those who opposed abolition were also able to point out the many excellent services such as music which would be lost when the ILEA was abolished.

Some Conservatives, however, saw the abolition of the ILEA as a first step towards abolishing all LEAs. Caroline Cox, in a Hillgate Group publication (1987), proposed that 'Schools must be released from the control of local government and financed by direct grant from central funds'.

Other Provisions of the 1988 Act

There were a number of other matters mentioned in the Act, some of them simply tidying up procedures, such as the length of the school day (Section 115). Others were much more important. Together they added added up to the accumulation of over 400 new powers for the Secretary of State. Hence the accusation that the move towards centralization was going too far.

Even members of the Conservative Party objected: 'The Secretary of State has taken more powers under the Bill than any member of the Cabinet, more than my right honourable friends the Chancellor of the Exchequer, the Secretary of State for Defence, and the Secretary of State for Social Services' (Edward Heath quoted in Wragg, 1988, p. 16).

ERA (1988) in Context: The High Point of New Right Policies?

ERA is historically significant because it represents the culmination of a break with the consensus politics of education which had prevailed from 1944 to 1979. As part of the argument in favour of radical change, expert opinion — the educational establishment — was dismissed as 'the voice of the producers'; the Act was intended to switch power to the consumer, but within a more controlled system.

Clearly there was a need to make changes in the system which had developed after World War II. This was indicated by Callaghan in 1976, still within the context of consensus. Changes would have taken place in the 1980s irrespective of the political complexion of the government in power. The Yellow Book (DES, 1976) provided an embryo programme of reform for the 1980s, including national curriculum, assessment and standards, schooling and work, value for money and school effectiveness. There would have certainly been some kind of control over the curriculum. But what in fact happened after 1979 was a mixture of bureaucratic centralism and New Right ideologies concerned with reducing public expenditure (sometimes under the banner of monetarism), restricting the powers of bureaucrats and LEAs, and introducing market competition into education by means of consumerist rhetoric about parental choice.

There have been many criticisms of the ERA. The most serious include: first, diminishing the power and influence of LEAs; second, threatening the idea of partnership on which the education system in the twentieth century had been based; third, replacing planning by market forces and consumer choice. The problem that remains for future planners and decision-makers is to what extent will it be necessary to unscramble some of the ERA provisions, or will it be possible to make the best of the post-1988 system and build on from there.

I suggested at the beginning of this chapter that it would not be wise to look for ideological coherence throughout the Act. Others have also pointed out this lack of coherence. David Coulby (1989) has written about no fewer than six ideological contradictions: the contradiction between vocationalism and traditional knowledge, between freedom and control, between local and central control, nationalism and internationalism, special educational needs and national needs, populist capitalism and state power.

The ERA was an ambitious attempt at radical change. It is

unlikely to provide the basis of lasting education reform for at least two reasons, one tactical, the other strategic. The tactical mistakes were to attempt to do too much, too quickly, without sufficient involvement of the teaching profession — the agenda was political rather than educational. The strategic errors were more fundamental, and connected with the ideological contradictions referred to above. One result is that the LEA partnership system has been seriously damaged without having a satisfactory alternative to replace it. Even if choice and the market could, eventually, make LEAs unnecessary, it will take time, and meanwhile there will be a danger of severe disruption, maybe collapse, in some LEAs.

I want to argue that the future of reform lies not with the kind of conflict generated by New Right ideologies, but from a new kind of consensus. This will be explored in chapters 7 and 8. It will be necessary to move forward from the 1988 ERA, not to pretend that we can revert to the education service as it was in 1979. It will be important to forge a consensus out of the 1988 Act, however imperfect it may have been. Before discussing that, it will be useful to review educational events 1988–91 (chapter 5) and then to examine carefully the concept of choice (chapter 6), before deciding on the part 'choice' might play in a consensus plan.

Appendix

Education Acts 1979–88	More Power to Parents Less for LEAs
1979 Education Act	Repealed 1976 Act (compelling LEAs to have comprehensive plans)
1980 Education Act	Assisted Places Scheme
	All independent schools to be registered
	Parents' right to choose school
	Parents' right to be represented on governing body
	LEAs and governors required to provide information on examination results, criteria for admission etc.
	Greater control over Advanced FE pool (capping)
	Restricted LEA rights to refuse places to outsiders
1981 Education Act	Following the Warnock Report (1978) LEAs given responsibilities for special education; parents given right to be consulted and to appeal against LEA
1984 Education (Grants and Awards) Act	Allowed government to allocate money to LEAs for specific purposes (reducing LEA control over grant)
1986 Education Act	LEATGS (GRIST)
1986 Education (No. 2) Act	Required every maintained school to have governing body
	Set formula for numbers of representatives on governing body; parents' representation strengthened
	Governors required to present

	annual report to parents and arrange meeting to discuss it
	Corporal punishment abolished in state schools
	Governors responsible for policy on sex education and for preventing political indoctrination
	Governors responsible for policy document on curriculum which could modify LEA policy
1987 Teachers' Pay and Conditions Act	Abolished Burnham
1988 Local Government Act	Clause 28 forbids local authorities to 'promote teaching in any maintained schools on the acceptability of homosexuality as a pretended family relationship'
1988 ERA	Open enrolment
	GMS
	etc.

Chapter 5

Events Since 1988

Disraeli declared that the fate of the country depended on education, and almost every subsequent Prime Minister has echoed that sentiment. But it only seems to galvanise us into action just about every thirty or forty years. The 1870 Education Act established universal education in England and Wales. Balfour's Education Act came in 1902, and Butler's Act in 1944. Now we are embarked on an even more radical series of reforms, which began in the 1980s and are continuing into the 1990s. Some people might feel tempted to say 'Look: we're not daft. We know about the importance of education. We knew there was a lot to be done. But you've been in power for over a decade. Why haven't you done it?'. . .(speech made by the Prime Minister, John Major, to the Centre for Policy Studies, Cafe Royal, 3 July 1991)

The Education Reform Act (1988) was the high point of education legislation during the Thatcher years. It was a major Act with far-reaching results. But it was seriously flawed: it left much undone, and a good deal of what was achieved had to be modified soon afterwards. In this chapter, in order to make an assessment about what has been achieved so far and what kind of consensus might be possible, I want to look at four kinds of 'unfinished business' 1988 to 1991:

(i) Education and training 16–19
(ii) Higher Education

(iii)   The National Curriculum and Assessment
(iv)   Aspects of choice: LMS, GMS and CTCs

Education and Training 16–19

One of the important areas untouched by ERA was the difficult question of providing for young people after the completion of compulsory schooling — the 16–19 age group. The main problem was that the majority of pupils left school at 16, many of them destined to receive *no* further education or training.

The GCE 'A' level route (for 18-year-old students) is very academic, abstract and often lacking relevance. The excuse for this has been that 'A' level was designed mainly as preparation for higher education (although by no means all successful candidates proceed to HE). At the other end of the spectrum of ability, we have an unacceptably large percentage of young people at work or unemployed with inferior training facilities or no facilities at all. Compared with many other advanced countries we are not doing well: we have only about half the percentage receiving education or training as the USA, Japan or the Netherlands. A related criticism is that there are unnecessary barriers between academic 'A' level courses and the more vocationally oriented programmes such as BTEC.

The main entry requirement for university in England and Wales is two passes at 'A' level. The typical programme for an 'A' level candidate will be three 'A' level subjects plus some kind of 'General Studies' which is usually not examined and therefore taken less seriously. For many years this narrow, often over-specialized curriculum has been criticized by educationists as well as employers. (There is nothing to prevent a candidate taking, for example, sociology, politics and economics, or Latin, French and German). Not only is the academic diet very unbalanced, it is also a part of a failure system. Although only the most able 16-year-old students begin 'A' level courses, about a quarter of them are destined to fail to achieve a pass of any kind after two years study. They have literally nothing to show for their two years' full-time course — no transcript of programmes followed, no credit transferable to other courses — they simply fail.

Background to the 'A' level problem

'A' level, together with the General Certificate of Education (GCE) 'O' level came into existence in 1951. Something like it had been recommended by the Norwood Report (1943), but as early as 1954, dissatisfaction was being expressed with the new arrangements. The Early Leaving Report (1954) expressed concern about the large number of able young people who left school at age 16 or even earlier. This was seen as a loss of opportunity to the individuals as well as a wastage of talent for the nation. Much the same message came through in the Crowther Report (1959) which indicated that the education service for the 15–18 age group was lagging behind other social and economic changes. I mention the 1954 and 1959 reports because, although the figures have changed, the major problem today is still that too few of all our young people are properly educated and trained.

Apart from the failure of the system to attract sufficient young people to continue into FE or HE there was another problem: the 'A' level structure of two, three or even four 'A' levels was producing young people who were over-specialized and lacking a broad balanced education. In the early 1960s there were attempts by the schools themselves to overcome the danger of over-specialization: a large number of schools with sixth forms agreed to broaden the curriculum by insisting on at least 25 per cent of the timetable being devoted to non-'A' level studies (the Agreement to Broaden the Curriculum (ABC)). Another aspect of the problem at that time was that universities were faced with increasing demand for HE — partly as a result of the bulge in the post-war birth rate, partly the success of the 1944 Act and secondary education for all. Universities reacted — somewhat unimaginatively — by controlling access to HE by demanding higher and higher grades at 'A' level. Hence the ABC — an agreement to resist the temptation for schools to become 'A' level factories. But the ABC faded away after a few years of good intentions.

In 1963 the Robbins Report recommended expanding HE. This was expected to solve the problem of the increasing demand for HE, but the supply of additional places, although considerable in universities and in the new polytechnics, failed to keep pace with the increasing demand. The rat race for higher and higher 'A' level grades continued, and with it the tendency for young people to concentrate more and more on their 'A' level subjects at the expense of a good general education.

In 1964 the Schools Council for Curriculum and Examinations was established, and one of its first priorities was to solve the 'A' level problem. The Council in 1966 came up with the idea of a broader and more balanced curriculum by replacing the three 'A' level pattern by two major subjects, two minor subjects plus General Studies. This met with some support and the Schools Council in 1968/69 suggested a two-stage structure: Qualifying and Further (Q and F). The idea was that able young people would take about eight 'O' levels, then in the first year of the sixth form take about five subjects at 'Q' level and only then specialize in, say, three subjects at 'F' level in their final year. This idea was rejected in 1969.

The main objection to Q and F was that it would involve major public examinations three years in succession (at age 16, 17 and 18). So the Schools Council in 1973 began working on an alternative proposal: a mixture of Normal and Further Levels (N and F), all of which would be taken at the end of the second year in the sixth form (thus avoiding an examination at age 17). The examining boards developed syllabuses and piloted them, only to be told in 1979 that universities would be unwilling to accept the lower standards involved without a longer university course. In 1980 there was a half-hearted attempt to revive the idea of 'Intermediate Levels', thus preserving the 'A' level standard. But the DES rejected that too.

So in 1984 the DES itself proposed the final solution: 'A' levels should remain at their well-known high standard, but be supplemented by courses *at the same standard*, requiring only half the content and study time. Advanced Supplementary (AS) was born — or at least conceived. The intention was that 'AS' would be used partly to contrast with 'A' levels and partly to complement 'A' level subjects in a way which would provide a broader curriculum by means of four subjects and perhaps even more.

To complicate the 16–18 scene there was another problem which had been developing since the 1950s, but especially after the institution of the Certificate of Secondary Education (CSE) in 1965 — 'the new sixth form'.

There were now students who wanted to continue studying beyond 16 but were regarded as 'insufficiently academic' for 'A' level courses. They may not have done very well at GCE or CSE at 16, but they were still keen to go on and could certainly benefit from further study. What could the school offer? A variety of vocational qualifications were available, but none of them was really suitable. Schools and examinations boards devised a Certificate of Extended Education (CEE) in 1976. Eventually a committee was set up to look at CEE — the Keohane Committee — which reported in 1979 and suggested a broad-based, common course structure. This did not meet with DES approval. The CEE was abolished and replaced by the Certificate of Pre-Vocational Education (CPVE) in 1983. CPVE was also a common core examination but more vocationally oriented. In 1986 the National Council for Vocational Qualifications (NCVQ) was established to coordinate and preserve standards in the 'jungle' of vocational courses.

That was the rather confusing picture in the mid-1980s. A picture to be made even more complex by the National Curriculum (ERA, 1988) and the GCSE (first examined in 1988) which was a common examination for the 16+ age group, involving more practical work, school-based work and course work of various kinds — all of which would have implications for 'A' level and other courses 16–19.

Higginson (1988) and After

To cast some light on the 16–19 problem, especially 'A' and 'AS', the government set up a small committee chaired by Dr. Gordon Higginson, Vice-Chancellor of the University of Southampton. They looked at the evidence, including the need for a broader curriculum, and proposed a five-subject structure: the five to be made up of a mixture of 'AS' and 'A' (but the 'A' levels would be leaner and tougher, i.e., less detailed content but just as demanding in other respects).

Although this proposal would not have solved all the problems 16–18 (it would still have been possible to take five subjects but no maths and science, for example) it met with a great deal of approval, including the support of Vice-Chancellors. But the Conservative government vetoed the main recommendation of a five subject package: 'A' level was regarded as the 'gold standard' which had to be preserved at all costs.

By this time (1988), the Schools Council had been abolished and replaced by the SEC and after the ERA (1988) by the SEAC. The SEAC was given the task of finding a solution to 'AS', 'A' levels and other problems at 16–19. Before handing over the task to the SEAC, the DES held a conference in November 1989. It was an optimistic occasion, giving the impression that at last there was a real intention to produce a reformed system.

Angela Rumbold, then Minister of State for Education, made an important speech in which she stressed four points. First, she claimed that there was already a healthy trend towards more balanced courses. Nearly one-third of 'A' level students were choosing a mixed diet. 'AS' courses were intended to accelerate that trend. But a mixture of 'A' and 'AS' will not be enough. There are other gaps to be filled such as numeracy, information technology and so on — it might be necessary to have a list of core skills for all the 16–19 age group (the NCC was then working on a list of core skills to be incorporated into all 16–19 studies).

The second point made by the Minister was that the present failure rate was too high: about 25 per cent on average for all subjects, and with about 10 per cent of all candidates achieving no 'A' level grades and having nothing to show after two years' study. In addition, there is an unquantified drop-out rate. The Minister asked what could be done to avoid that kind of failure — without lowering standards?

Third, should there be more opportunity for movement between 'A' level courses and vocational courses and qualifications? Including provision for credit transfer?

Fourth, more young people were needed in training and education 16 to 19. The CBI had suggested 50 per cent achieving NVQ Level III (that is, the equivalent of five GCSE and two 'A' levels).

All of Mrs. Rumbold's four points were valid, but they made 'A' and 'AS' reform even more complex. The problem is not only broadening the curriculum, but also improving access and including new skills. All without lowering standards! How?

The real question in 1988 was whether 'A/AS' could be tidied up and offered as one route with vocational courses as a second route? Or did both need radical reform and integration? Since Higginson the balance of opinion has overwhelmingly been in favour of something broader and more balanced than 'A/AS' (at least five subjects plus core skills). There has also been a clear preference among educationists and industrialists not for two routes but for integration and flexibility — i.e., some form of common qualification, at least at 17 before the final choice. Since 1988 a number of individuals and organizations became committed to that view.

In April 1990, Sir John Cassells produced a report for the Policy Studies Institute (PSI) *Britain's Real Skill Shortage* which recommended a new qualification at 'A' level standard covering academic and vocational, full-time and part-time. In May 1990 Sir Christopher Ball wrote *More Means Different* on behalf of the RSA stressing the need to widen access to HE and questioning the usefulness of 'A' levels.

The debate continued throughout 1991: in April the Secondary Heads Association published a report *16–19 The Way Forward* which suggested five foundation subjects (with a qualification) in the first year, and in year 2 a choice 'A/AS' (three-five subjects) or Advanced Vocational Courses with a modular/credit transfer structure. In the same month the Committee of Vice-Chancellors and Principals (CVCP) expressed their preference for a radical long-term solution. At about the same time, the Association of Principals of Sixth Form Colleges (APVIC) submitted a document recommending a national post-16 framework with a single award (which would include 'A/AS', BTEC and others). In May the Royal Society declared that 'A' level was irrelevant to industry and HE, and should be replaced by an Advanced Certificate and Diploma (*Beyond GCSE*, 1991).

The Conservative politicians, however, remained committed to the two-route approach: Margaret Thatcher in an answer to a Parliamentary question in October 1990 indicated her support for 'A' level standards in their existing form; in November Kenneth Clarke promised the House of Commons that 'A' levels would remain the 'gold standard'; broadening the curriculum at 16+ would take other forms — better and more attractive vocational courses; in December Education Minister, Tim Eggar, speaking at a conference of science teachers, promised to retain Advanced Level standards but said the government wanted a large increase in the numbers staying on post-16 for vocational qualifications.

In 1991, Kenneth Clarke, speaking at the Annual Conference of ACFHE in February said that he intended to maintain the two pathways post-16 ('A' level and NVQ): 'It is the level of qualification that matters not whether it is academic or vocational'. He said that far higher numbers should reach NVQ levels 2 and 3, and that the 'A' level path and the NVQ path to higher education should be equally valued. It was clear that the government has decided against any kind of broad 'Baccalaureat' solution, and that 'A' levels should be kept separate.

The White Paper: Education and Training for the 21st Century (May 1991)

The White Paper *Education and Training for the 21st Century* was launched by the Prime Minister, John Major, in May 1991 in a blaze of publicity, but it was generally considered to be an unsatisfactory set of proposals. Even the *Financial Times*, normally a supporter of the government, was critical of the adequacy of the recommendations, and *The Independent* leader (21 May 1991) was headed 'Timid Tory Plan for Training'.

The main failing of the White Paper had been predicted: the Conservative government was unwilling to change 'A' levels — 'the gold standard'. Apart from a predeliction for the status quo, the continued existence of 'A' levels has the advantage of enabling universities in England and Wales (not Scotland) to continue to have first degree courses which take only three years full-time study to complete — the shortest degree course of high quality in the world. But the price paid for this express route is a high one — narrow specialism and lack of flexibility. There are very poor arrangements to transfer in or out of 'A' level courses.

The White Paper solution was essentially to preserve 'A'

levels, to encourage 'AS' as a means of introducing breadth and to develop vocational courses for non-'A' level young people which would be different from but equivalent to 'A' level in terms of prestige and access.

The fallacy on which the White Paper was built was that the circle could be squared by playing the 'parity of esteem' card. But one of the lessons that should have been learned from secondary education in the 1950s was precisely that in a very class-conscious and status-conscious society it is impossible to say that although 'A' level courses will lead to high prestige jobs, vocational courses leading to less prestigious positions will be 'different but equal'. Just as comprehensive schools were necessary — socially and academically — in the 1960s, and were eventually accepted by the Conservative Party as necessary, so some kind of comprehensive structure 16–19 was needed in 1991. The perpetuation of narrow, exclusive courses cannot be sustained in educational or vocational terms. Much more flexibility and interrelating is needed with a blurring of the distinction between academic and vocational.

It is not an easy task, but several models had been offered before May 1991: for example, in July 1990 the Institute for Public Policy Research (IPPR) recommended a much more radical reform on the grounds that tinkering with the present system would be doomed to failure. *A British 'Baccalaureat': Ending the Division Between Education and Training* (IPPR, 1990) recommended that 'A' level and vocational courses should be abolished and that all young people would study in tertiary colleges three areas: social and human sciences; natural sciences and technology; and arts, language and literature. Such a course would be much closer to what is required in many European countries and is similar in some respects to the requirements of the International Baccalaureat.

The government, however, shied away from that kind of radical solution. Right-wing ideology and many independent schools demanded the retention of the existing structure with minor modifications but with no complete integration. Instead, we were offered a list of overall aims which were unobjectionable in aspiration but extremely vague in terms of practicality. There was much reference to the need for 'cultural change' but little guidance on how to achieve it. Had such a list of aims been produced by a university it would have been instantly dismissed as 'ivory tower'. The White Paper proposes an extension of provision of vocational courses and their upgrading to standards to be set by NCVQ. The aim is to provide all 16–17-year-old school leavers with a training credit (or voucher) worth about £1000 by 1996. The Training and Enterprise Councils (TECs) will also cooperate in the organization of training. Training credit vouchers had been piloted on an experimental basis in ten areas since April 1991; so confident were John Major and Kenneth Clarke of the principle, that, without waiting for the results of evaluation studies, they immediately set up training credits on a national basis.

The problem of education and training for 16–19 remained unsolved. An opportunity had been missed. It would have to be an item for the consensus agenda.

Higher Education

One of the stranger features of British higher education is the barrier — the binary line — between universities and other institutions of higher education including polytechnics, some of whose reputation is very high. Other countries may have a more or less obvious 'pecking order' in terms of prestige but only the UK has such a rigid distinction. The origins of the binary line have more to do with questions of financial control than academic distinction.

In 1963 the Robbins Report recommended a vast expansion of HE, partly by creating new universities, partly by upgrading non-university institutions to full university status. This involved some which had been controlled and financed via LEAs transferring to UGC funding. It would at that time — in the 1960s — have been possible to have created a unified, national system of HE funded by UGC. The DES perceived one disadvantage in this: universities had a tendency to do whatever they liked (despite their dependence, indirectly, on government funds). The civil servants thought that there might be an advantage in keeping some HE outside the UGC system, maintain the fiction of control by LEAs, but in reality for the DES to keep a tighter financial hold on all developments. Thus Crosland in 1966 was persuaded to adopt the idea of a 'binary system' which he announced in his famous Woolwich speech. Crosland himself later claimed to have regretted embarking upon a policy which had the unintended consequence of reinforcing the notion that universities were high status, concerned with knowledge for its own sake, whereas polytechnics were utilitarian, concerned mainly with vocational courses, and of lower status, having their degrees awarded by the Council for National Academic Awards (CNAA) rather than on the authority of their own royal charter.

The artificial distinction was compounded by the differences in funding arrangements whereby the UGC made grants to universities on the assumption that every university teacher was also a researcher, whereas no such assumption was made about staff in polytechnics, although some of them did good research.

There were many other inconsistencies in the binary system. For example, HMI could demand admittance to polytechnics but not into universities. The binary system was overdue for reform by the time of ERA (1988). The Act, however, only tackled part of the problem, and as I suggested in chapter 4, managed both to antagonize universities and to fail to satisfy the needs of the other side of the line as well as the LEAs which nominally controlled them. The main result of ERA was that polytechnics were taken away from LEA control and were financed by the new PCFC on a national basis. Many predicted that it would only be a matter of time before UFC and PCFC were combined to fund a national system of HE.

A further step in that direction came about with the publication of a White Paper on the same day as the White Paper on Education and Training 16–19.

The White Paper: Higher Education: A New Framework
(May, 1991) Cm 1541

The main proposal of the White Paper is the abolition of the binary line. This was undoubtedly a correct decision, but it was — curiously — justified in terms of competition: institutions were expected to expand by competing for funds and students, and it was therefore desirable that this competition should not be artificially constrained by the binary distinction.

Many right-wing advisors (and some Vice-Chancellors) had long recommended that the funding of HE should be reduced to a simple matter of payment to the university of tuition fees by the students themselves. Universities and polytechnics would earn income by recruiting students who would pay the full cost fee (some of which might be covered by grants or loans). This solution was, however, rejected in the White Paper on the grounds that the government might want to 'steer' HE and reward quality. (So much for faith in the efficiency of the market!) A single funding structure for all HE was proposed, and all institutions would compete on an equal basis.

Similarly, there had been suggestions that the government should abolish the 'dual support' system of funding research, whereby universities (but not polytechnics) receive research funds as part of an institutional grant and also compete for project grants from research councils. The attempt by the UFC to move away from the dual system had run into difficulties, so the temptation to abolish dual funding was resisted, at least at this stage, whilst moving a little further in the direction of funding by research contracts. The funding councils would meanwhile still be responsible for distributing research funds *selectively* but HE institutions would be expected to be much more accountable for the research monies received — a not unreasonable requirement. (Under the pre-1988 UGC system all tenured university staff were assumed to spend 30–40 per cent of their time on research, but were not required to show what they did with that time.) Another solution to the research/teaching problem might have been the US practice of giving some staff 'teaching only' contracts for a notional 75 per cent of a year. This was not adopted in the White Paper, but it may be taken up by individual institutions.

Whilst funding will no longer be separated into university and non-university, regional funding will be developed by having three HE funding councils — one each for England, Wales and Scotland (with Northern Ireland kept in close relationship). The tradition, since 1988, of having a high percentage of members of the funding committee from industry and commerce will continue. The government acknowledges its major responsibility for funding HE but encourages institutions to seek more funds from industry and elsewhere.

In the midst of much rhetoric about competition, and an implicit commitment to market forces, proposals were set out for much greater control of HE. A new key term of art was 'Quality Assurance' — another dimension of accountability. Paragraph 60 of the White Paper sub-divides quality assurance in the following way:

(i)   Quality control (mechanisms within institutions)
(ii)   Quality audit (external scrutiny of internal control)
(iii)   Validation (approval of courses by a validating body)
(iv)   Accreditation (CNAA delegation of responsibility to institutions)
(v)   Quality assessment (external review of quality of teaching and learning)

Maurice Kogan's fears (1989) about 'managerialism' (see chapter 4, p. 56) appear to have been justified. In the context of the discussion of quality assurance it was proposed that the CNAA be abolished, but that there should be a Quality Audit Unit (QAU) for each funding council (staffed partly by HMI). It was also proposed that performance indicators would have a more significant part to play. Part of the function of the QAU would be to make available information about institutions to potential students and employers (the HE equivalent of schools having to publish assessment and examinations results).

The proposals are neatly summarized in paragraph 87.

QUALITY ASSURANCE IN HIGHER EDUCATION

	CURRENT ARRANGEMENTS		PROPOSED ARRANGEMENTS
	Universities	*Polytechnics and colleges*	*All HE*
Quality Control	Institutions	Institutions	Institutions
Quality Audit	Academic Audit Unit (CVCP)	CNAA	Single quality audit unit independent of HE Funding Councils
Validation	Self-validation	Effective self-validation for some; university or CNAA for others	Degree awarding institutions

Quality Assessment			
For HE Funding Councils	Subject	HMI	QAUs for each new Council
For Secretaries of State	UFC	HMI	New HE Funding Councils

Much of this could form part of a new consensus on HE. Whilst some aspects of control may appear to be a little heavy-handed, it has to be recognized that for a long time universities have been in a privileged position and have not always matched privilege with responsibility. The decision to abolish the binary line is a good one, and will remove such anomalies as HMI having the right of access to polytechnics but not to universities.

However, the White Paper is essentially a bureaucratic document — tidying up controls, but having no real solutions to offer on the two main problems. The first problem is the low participation rate: it is assumed that — somehow — greater competition will result in a higher percentage of young people entering HE (up to one in three by the year 2000), but apart from more competition no other guidance is offered. Similarly, there is no vision of greater access for working class young people and those from some ethnic minorities — the other main problem.

The problems of HE have been partially dealt with, but there are still outstanding questions of access and funding which must be addressed. In particular the conflict between market mechanisms and planning needs to be carefully thought out. I will return to these issues in Chapters 7 and 8.

National Curriculum Assessment (NCA)

Changes to the national curriculum and its assessment have been of three kinds — political, bureaucratic and professional.

In chapter 4 I described how some educationists were critical of the national curriculum for its unjustified subject structure, but approved of the model of assessment proposed by TGAT. Part of the attraction of the ten-level model was that it envisaged assessment in formative, as well as summative, terms — teachers could use assessment materials as part of their teaching programme and use the results for diagnostic purposes. The major disadvantage was that the results at age 11 and 14 were to be published for reasons of parental choice and competition.

As the assessment materials were developed and piloted, it became clear that some Conservative politicians, including the Secretary of State, Kenneth Clarke, simply did not approve of the complex nature of the assessment materials. He referred to them on one occasion as 'elaborate nonsense'. By the summer of 1991 all the education Ministers had expressed a preference for short-written tests, and John Major's speech to the CPS in July 1991 reinforced the message. The clash between the DES politicians and the SEAC intensified until, on 15 July 1991, Philip Halsey, the Chairman, announced his 'early retirement', and was replaced by Brian Griffiths (who had been created Lord Griffiths by Margaret Thatcher), a Professor of Economics well known for his reactionary views on education. Political conflict was intensified.

The views of DES bureaucrats in this dispute were not made public, but it was clear that some senior officials were by now advocates of 'choice and competition' and did not support their SEAC colleagues as strongly as they might have. They also had a NCA agenda to cope with: the DES had been warned that the structure of attainment targets in maths and science was so complex (fourteen ATs in maths, seventeen in science) that the GCSE groups, represented by the Joint Council, could not guarantee continuity of standards for the 1994 examination which by then would have been converted from the A–G grading to the ten-level system demanded by the NC. The bureaucratic solution was to recommend that the number of ATs in science and maths should come closer to the five in English which were found to be more manageable by teachers (and it was hoped by GCSE examiners).

These bureaucratic aims did not necessarily conflict with the education priorities, but the pace demanded was not sensible — the timing was necessary for a political agenda rather than educational requirements.

The teachers did not initially resist these changes. They too were victims of the rushed political agenda and found themselves trying out hastily prepared assessment materials after inadequate training. The result was that at Key Stage 1 they complained about the amount of time that was necessary for testing, and in July 1991 a joint delegation of teachers and parents demanded the abolition of testing at 7, to be replaced by reliance on teacher assessment. This was refused, but a promise was given that tests in future would be simpler. The professionals had, unintentionally, played into the hands of the politicians and bureaucrats.

The point of describing these events of 1991 in some detail is to indicate the danger of education matters being politicized. Unnecessary conflict was generated in 1988–91 because a potentially useful education reform was made to fit a political ideology with an impossible timetable.

This problem also remains unsolved. There is a clash of interest on NCA between teachers who want to use assessment for the benefit of pupils and politicians who see NCA as part of market choice. TGAT had attempted to bridge the gap, but was not completely successful. A renewed effort will be necessary in order to find a consensus solution.

Aspects of Choice: LMS, GMS, CTCs

The short-term effect of these reforms was not to give schools and parents more choice but to threaten the existence of LEAs. The sections of ERA concerning LMS were intended to transfer part of the LEA budget to the schools. This was not in itself reprehensible, but LEAs were often left with a budget insufficient to maintain services such as special needs, school psychologists, orchestras and many others which were better provided on a regional basis.

Added to this problem was the increasing tendency of politicians to encourage more schools to opt out of LEA control, taking a further slice of the LEA budget with them. By the summer of 1991 some LEAs — including some Tory counties — were not sure that they could continue. Others were accused by politicians of obstructing the move towards GMS. And CTCs, in the few places where they existed, were creaming off some of the more able pupils, leaving the LEA comprehensive schools, less and less viable at a time of declining rolls.

Another aspect of 'choice' (or non-choice) began to be publicized in the press — the inability of parents to be given a place in the schools they chose for their children. The Consumers' Association reported a 30 per cent increase nationally in official parental complaints about not being given a place in a school of their choice (and in some areas it was twice as high). *The Guardian* took a particular interest in this issue, and on 16 July 1991 reported the example of a boy in Hertfordshire whose parents had chosen the comprehensive school in walking distance of his home, but because the school was now open to 'parental choice', he was unable to be accommodated and had to travel to a school eleven miles away around the M25 with a bus service which he had to pick up three miles from his home. This was said to be not an isolated case.

All this suggested that whatever the key might be to a reformed system, it did not seem to be 'choice'. Yet in John Major's speech to the CPS at the Cafe Royal on 3 July 1991, choice was still the main theme. It was an important speech in which John Major gave four answers to the question he himself raised (which I quoted at the head of this chapter) — that is, why after more than ten years of Conservative government had the education problems not been solved? The four answers given by the Prime Minister were: first, that we have a long history of indifference — even hostility — to education deep in our culture, and cultural change takes time; second, that the Conservative governments had made a bold beginning with TVEI, CTCs, GMS etc; third, the government had spent more money (per pupil) but could not itself raise standards — others must play their part; and finally, it was important to preserve traditional values whilst pursuing innovation — back to the idea of cultural changes needing time. All of this would have been quite reasonable — especially the point about the difficulty of changing the culture. But these four answers were not related to the second half of the speech which concentrated on the government strengthening the route to GMS and therefore choice. John Major seemed unaware of the problems raised by choice, and spoke only of the supposed advantages of choice. Much the same is true of the Citizens' Charter which appeared a little later — too much is claimed for what choice can realistically achieve and no mention is made of the problems outlined earlier in this chapter. The speech and the Citizens' Charter are concerned with consumer choice rather than with overall quality.

Underlying this difficulty there is a confusion about the meaning of choice and the implications of basing policy on choice. Reverting to my own earlier classification, I would suggest that privatizers see choice as the only necessary mechanism; minimalists see choice as a partial answer (some can choose and benefit from choice; those who cannot, have an inferior system where choice plays a much less important part); Pluralists want choice, but do not see it as the main factor — the public planned system must be as good as the private choice system, but planning is as important as choice; Comprehensive planners would not emphasize choice, believing that a good planned system should provide what everyone needed.

The logic of John Major's emphasis on parental choice is that it leads to minimalism — choice will provide better for those who can pay and for parents who choose 'wisely' and have their choices met, but it will leave some with unfulfilled desires, and more importantly, will leave some worse off. This kind of minimalism is difficult to reconcile with the Prime Minister's declared intention to provide equality of opportunity. John Major's 'choice' is not the pure choice of the privatizers but the limited choice of consumerism. Conservatives like John Major, and presumably Kenneth Clarke, wanted choice not only because they believe in market mechanisms, but also because they felt that education had got into the wrong hands — left-wing LEAs and experts (the producers) rather than parents and industrialists. The move towards CTCs and GMS is also an attempt to redress that balance. But there is another fallacy here: parents and industrialists are not the consumers of education — the whole of society should have a right to participate in the educational debate. Education should not be regarded as a consumer-commodity to be bought and sold in the market place, but as a social service. The main question is not to increase choice but to improve the whole service.

By June 1991 Vernon Bogdanor and other Conservatives had spotted this fallacy (particularly in the context of LEA planning). Bogdanor wanted to reduce the emphasis on market choice and, using Albert Hirschman's terminology, to stress the importance of 'voice' rather than 'exit'. In a democracy it is important to encourage 'voice' — i.e., vocal participation — and only use 'exit' (choice to go elsewhere) as a very last resort. Ironically, Major's Citizens' Charter also recognizes the importance of 'voice' in principle — with a totally free market a Charter would be bureaucratic nonsense. A Citizens' Charter only makes sense in a mixed economy where voice is important. But what kind of mix? What is the best relationship between choice and planning, exit and voice? Bogdanor was, of course, not the first to use Hirschman's thesis in this way. Stewart Ranson (1990) had warned of these dangers immediately after the 1988 Act had been passed.

John Major spoke as if he believed that introducing more choice would produce the kind of deep cultural change that was needed. But if choice makes any kind of difference it will be superficial rather than reaching the deep structures of our society. Even allowing for the nature of his audience, the Prime Minister might have been expected to delve more deeply into the issue of choice. No mention was made, for example, of the important Scottish evidence (*Parental Choice and Educational Policy* by Adler, Petch and Tweedie (1989) which describes the losses, as well as the gains, involved in increasing parental choice.

Chapter 6 will examine arguments about choice and the market in some detail. Meanwhile by 1991 it was already clear that too much had been claimed for choice, and that 'exit' had been over-sold. A consensus approach will need to investigate the most appropriate mixtures of exit and voice — choice and active participation.

Problems of Choice, the Market and Educational Planning

So, choice and accountability are key concepts of Conservative philosophy which underpin current education
policy. They can be the means of giving good schools the
opportunity to become even better; but more importantly,
they can give greater power and influence to those parents
and pupils who are the most vulnerable and whom the
present system is failing. Power to the people. Fairer and
more democratic policies. These are our concerns. (Cox,
1988)

'Choice' is one of those words that demands approval — it is
difficult to be against choice in principle although it may not be
possible to deliver it in practice. For anyone to be against choice
in principle puts him/her into the category of 'knowing better'
than the chooser — a position correctly adopted by parents of
young children but one which has to be modified as the children
grow older unless there is some kind of utopian vision of what
is best for everyone. Karl Popper has warned us about the dangers of that position. But Libertarians and followers of Hayek go
to the other extreme and would settle everything by choice and
the market — the hidden hand is always better than a planned
solution. For many commodities — for *adults* — the market may
work better than any other, but not necessarily for all public
services, and certainly not where children are the choosers. Few
Libertarians believe that children should be allowed to choose
everything for themselves.

Choice in the context of education is highly problematic, and not the simple matter it is sometimes suggested by those on the right. This chapter will attempt to deal with two issues: first, what is the function of choice in education? Second, can good quality education, including desirable choices, be best offered by a planned system or by market competition?

'Choice' is a fashionable slogan word in the rhetoric of the New Right, some of whom claim that more choice automatically means better quality; another assumption is that because some kinds of choice are desirable, then all (or at least most) kinds of choice should be catered for. Both of these assumptions need to be questioned. The claim that choice means quality is based on a number of quite different factors: at one level the connection between a school and quality is based on the free market idea that parents would choose good schools, thereby eventually closing down poor schools. At a different level, the idea of pupils choosing what they want to study is alleged to improve their motivation. Clearly these are very different kinds of choice.

It may be helpful to begin the analysis by looking at areas which have been declared by Acts of Parliament to be 'non-choice': compulsory attendance at school 5 to 16, and, since the ERA (1988), a compulsory national curriculum for *state* schools. Extreme Libertarians would, of course, object to both of those on the grounds that the state has no business to interfere in that area of personal decision-making. I will return to that issue later. For the moment I simply want to note that legislation has been passed, and to look at the reasoning behind those laws, both of which involve a restriction of liberty — a denial of choice — for children and their parents.

The reasoning behind both examples of non-choice is complex. In the case of compulsory schooling there is an implicit intention to give what are considered to be children's '*needs*' higher priority than parental choice. If all parents could be relied upon to make satisfactory arrangements for their children's education, then compulsion would be unnecessary. Because this is thought not to be the case, children are given legal protection against their own parents' apathy, fecklessness or stupidity. For obvious reasons that justification for the legislation is nowhere spelt out quite so frankly, but the principle is clear: schooling is considered to be so high a priority — perhaps even a human right — that it overrides choice. An extension of the reasoning behind compulsion is that the state has a duty or responsibility to provide schooling of a reasonable quality, and that every child has a right or entitlement to schooling of a certain quality. It would be a strange law which made something compulsory but made no attempt to define what it was in terms of content and quality — hence the National Curriculum.

If the case is so straightforward then why was there no national curriculum from 1944 to 1988? The answer would seem to be that an assumption was made in the 1940s that there was general agreement — consensus — about what should go on in schools, and that therefore it was unnecessary to write it down. But it was only *partly* true in the 1940s that there was consensus about curriculum, and in the 1960s and 1970s the curriculum itself certainly became increasingly controversial. By 1988 some kind of national agreement on the curriculum was long overdue, given the legal requirement of compulsory schooling.

There is another aspect to the reasoning behind compulsion: the notion that education not only brings benefits to the individual, but that schooling of the right kind is advantageous to the community as a whole — producing better citizens, more caring parents, more efficient workers, fitter and better quality conscripts for the army, and so on. The motives are complex, and we should beware of some Marxist 'explanations' which declare that 'the only reason for state education is that capitalism needs. . .'. The history of education in most countries, certainly in the UK, reveals a multiplicity of factors behind the development of the state education system.

Even so, in a democratic society there is a delicate balance between wanting to respect parental choice, and the state needing to rely on the advice of its own experts. Libertarians of the left and the right argue that experts can be wrong and frequently disagree among themselves, so a safer policy would be to rely on a free market and parental choice. I shall, later in this chapter, argue that a free market in education is likely to be inferior to a system planned by professionals, because a free market is only efficient if there is 'perfect information' — or at least very good information — as well as the ability to pay. Many parents are not in a position to know what is on offer, nor to know how to judge its quality, nor to pay for what they would like. Given that situation, to talk of a free market is either naive or hypocritical; it can also be argued that what parents want may not always be in the best interests either of the children or of the community as a whole.

So we come down, perhaps a little reluctantly, on the side of compulsion. But in a democratic society we will be uneasy about invoking the powers of the state too readily. And, at present, a 'let out' is provided: parents who can afford a private school can opt out of the compulsory system; parents who cannot or do not wish to use a school can, in theory, educate their children at home. But for most parents there is no real choice. This accounts for a move in the USA — not confined to the political right — to try to extend the range of parental discretion, asking why should only the rich have the privilege of choosing a school? Why not extend choice of school to all parents by such devices as voucher systems? (see also Chubb and Moe, 1990, for an elaboration of this argument).

That brings us back to the need to try to analyze desirable and less desirable choices. There are a number of levels of choice involved:

(i) I have already mentioned the choice (for some) of deciding between state and private schools.

(ii) There is also the extension of choice of schools within the state system (by open enrolment, GMS and CTCs, which will be discussed later in this chapter).

(iii) Within any school some choices would be desirable — complete freedom of curriculum choice is not possible, but some variety within and beyond the National Curriculum is highly desirable. It is also important that individual differences in learning ability and learning styles are respected. This is very largely a matter of enlightened school organization and teacher professionalism. But within a school should children have a choice of teacher? This might, in practice, be much more important than parental choice of school! It is the kind of choice which is desirable but difficult to legislate for, and which is not catered for any better in private schools. The current situation where a pupil has to change schools in order to change teachers is a strange one. Later in this book I shall be looking at possible changes in school organization which would go some way towards reducing the importance of a dependency kind of teacher-pupil relationship. Teachers are important but it is at least arguable they should not be so dominant in the teaching-learning process; older pupils should take more control over their learning and come to regard teachers as additional resources rather than directors of the learning process (see chapter 8).

At this stage, having suggested that some choices are more important than others, and that not all choices are even desirable, I would now like to move on to the relationship between choice in education and the market. The most important observation to be made initially is that having choice is by no means the same as having a market (free or regulated): a market, or a quasi-market, might be one way of delivering certain kinds of choice, but some choices have nothing to do with the market (within a completely planned system some kinds of desirable choices can be made available). Finally, it needs to be acknowledged that an education system should not be preferred simply because it offers more choice. It must all depend on the importance or desirability of the choices offered.

In chapter 5 I suggested that one of the needs of the 1990s will be to revive the idea of partnership rather than to encourage more and more centralization. This is likely to be a point of policy agreed by all the major parties. But one of the problems facing partnership will be to reconcile, if reconciliation is possible, the existence of a central authority, LEAs and the idea of using 'the market' to deliver choice in education. It will be necessary to return to these issues later. Meanwhile, let us examine the range of possible relations between the state and 'the market' in education. There are, in theory at least, six possible policies:

(i) a completely free market in education — no state intervention;

   (ii)   a free market constrained and regulated by the state;

  (iii)   a school system which is wholly private but subsidized or completely paid for by the state;

  (iv)   a system where schools — state and private — are all in competition with each other (mixed economy, quasi-market);

   (v)   a state system and a private system complementing each other (mixed economy, planned);

  (vi)   a state system only — all independent schools abolished.

There are advantages and disadvantages for each possibility, although some might be ruled out fairly quickly.

Barr (1987), approaching the problem as an economist studying welfare, made a distinction between the amount of welfare (including education) which a society wishes to provide, and the means of delivering it. The first is a question open to ideological debate but the second is, or should be, a purely practical, or technical question of what is the most efficient method of delivering that amount of education. The position may be more complicated than that, but Barr's distinction is nevertheless an important one.

I will begin by discussing each of those six positions listed above, then proceed to outline the education services needed, before moving to a recommendation about which of the six policies might be the most efficient, or the most acceptable in our society in the 1990s.

Six Possible Policies on Market in Education

Option 1 — A Completely Free Market — No State Intervention

The most extreme free market position would be to allow the market unrestrained influence by abolishing state provision altogether. Education would be completely privatized and schools would be run as charities, trusts, private companies or in some other way. Parents would have complete freedom of choice within the constraint of their ability to pay. The state would have no involvement in maintaining standards or in financing schools directly or indirectly. Under such a system — or lack of a system — there would be no compulsory attendance at school.

Although a completely free market in education has been advocated by some on the extreme libertarian, laissez-faire, right-wing of the Conservative Party, it is difficult to envisage now because we have become so accustomed to state provision. But in the early nineteenth century this laissez-faire approach to education was the dominant view. It was not until 1833 that there was any state money spent on providing schools (and even then they were not state schools but schools provided by voluntary organizations). Since then more and more public money has been spent each year on education. We have to ask why if the free market is such a good idea, it was abandoned in 1833. The answer is that the free market system in the 1830s was failing to reach more than a very small proportion of the population at a time when it was desirable, for various reasons, to reach a much higher number. Times have changed, and we cannot simply assume that a free market system would not work now. But it has also to be said that no advanced industrial society operates with a system of education depending completely on private organizations. Those who advocate total privatization have not produced convincing arguments for returning to a completely free market system which has previously failed and cannot be shown to be working elsewhere.

There are many reasons why a free market would be unsatisfactory. Most parents would probably pay for schooling, but inequality of provision would be aggravated (i.e., the rich would buy more and better; some parents would buy little or nothing). There are other disadvantages such as economic inefficiency — a modern industrial society needs educated manpower. Moreover, most people now accept that there are good social, cultural and moral reasons for state investment in education: the nineteenth century laissez-faire view has almost completely disappeared.

Nicholas Barr (1987) writing about the economics of the welfare state in more general terms, came to this conclusion about education:

A pure market system is likely to be highly inefficient, and also inequitable to the extent that knowledge, power and access to capital markets are correlated with economic status. Unrestricted market provision of education is theoretically implausible and, in practice, does not exist in any country. (pp. 311–2)

Those who advocate a return to the market have ignored the fact that free markets are only efficient when there is perfect information available and perfect competition (or at least very good information and competition). This is not the case in education, and it is difficult to see how it could be.

A completely free market in education would be unfair to some individuals and economically inefficient for society as a whole. It has very few advocates.

Option 2 — A Market Constrained and Regulated by the State

The second possible use of the market would be to have a completely privatized system of schooling, but include some kind of state supervision. The supervision could take a variety of forms: the state could legislate for minimum standards, a National Curriculum, and insist that all teachers should be qualified; it could have a national inspectorate which would have the power to recommend the closure of schools not meeting required standards.

This arrangement has also been tried before in the UK, from 1839 to 1870, and found wanting. Matthew Arnold, one of the best of Her Majesty's Inspectors, was also a student of comparative education, and became convinced that the laissez-faire approach in England was causing us to lag behind our industrial competitors, particularly in those countries he had visited — France and Prussia — where he believed much superior, planned systems were developing. We should not simply assume that a privatized system, operating within state guidelines, supervised by HMI, would not work. But it is difficult to see why such a system would be better than one provided by the state.

One clear deficiency of the pre-1870 system was the 'patchiness' of provision — both in terms of covering the whole country, and in terms of differences in quality. In a privately provided system inspectors can insist on minimum standards, but they cannot compel a local community to provide a school, nor can they do much to encourage quality beyond the defined minimum.

There is also the problem of cash — in two ways. First, there is the difficulty about whether schools are a legitimate medium for profit-making. If proprietorial schools are permitted, there will be problems of 'reasonable' profit margins, giving inspectors a difficult task of detecting exploitation. Second, there is the problem that not all parents will be able to afford education of any reasonable quality. The danger would be more wastage of talent than there is now and a widening of the gap between the privileged and the less privileged.

Option 3 — A School System which is Wholly Private but Subsidized or Paid For by the State

In both the USA and the UK, some advocates of private schooling have suggested that a more efficient way of providing state support would be to pay for or subsidize private schools rather than attempting to provide and run schools by means of a centralized or decentralized bureaucratic machine. In the UK critics of the state system such as Stuart Sexton (1990) and many others, have advocated this alternative, paid for by voucher schemes. It seems to me that vouchers should be regarded as a mechanism for delivery — neither good nor bad in principle. I will, therefore, consider them in chapter 8.

The policy under consideration here is not vouchers but the possibility of a wholly private system paid for or subsidized by the state. Vouchers could be one way of achieving that but not the only one. The real point at issue is whether such a system would be more efficient than a planned state system. That suggestion is based on two assumptions: first, that private schools are likely to be more efficient, partly because they are free of LEA bureaucracy, and second, that if they are not efficient they will close down. These are, however, only assumptions made by those who dislike state provision: some very bad private schools survive for a long time, partly for reasons of lack of perfect information already referred to, and partly because some fee-paying parents are apathetic and slow to take action even when conditions are appalling.

Barr (1987) points out that the absence of 'perfect information' is particularly imporant in education:

> Private production is likely to be efficient only if its quality is adequately policed. Libertarians dispute this view, arguing that dissatisfied parents could move their child to another school, and that if a private school has a bad reputation it will go out of business. The weakness of this line of argument is two-fold. First, parents may not have sufficient information to realize that their child is being badly educated or, if they do, may not have the confidence to do anything about it. Second, education is not a repeatable experiment. It is true that a restaurant which provides bad service will go out of business; its former clients will have suffered nothing more than a bad meal, and can spend the rest of their lives going to better restaurants. But the application of this argument to education makes an unfounded leap in logic. Education is in large measure a once-and-for-all experience; a child who has had a year or two of bad education may never recover. In addition, a child may face a high emotional cost. . .in changing school. A more apt analogy is a restaurant which gives unknowing customers food so bad that it might cause permanent ill-health. (pp. 312–3)

One of the interesting features of education in England is that newspapers are much more likely to seize upon a state school scandal (such as William Tyndale) and generalize from that single example; but when quite horrifying conditions of sexual abuse or excessive corporal punishment are found in a private school, no such generalizations are made. The main point of contention is whether it is easier to eliminate 'disasters' under state ownership with direct control, or by allowing the market to operate. There is no evidence that the market eliminates all bad practice — i.e., that communication of information is quicker and more effective in a market situation than in a planned system.

There would seem to be no argument in favour of privatizing the whole education service. Had the English education system developed in a different way historically, then there might be arguments for retaining a wholly private system, subsidized but with strict regulations and control. But since this is not the case, we should be very wary about embarking upon a radical change of this kind without fully considering all the disadvantages, some of which will be the same as encouraging 'open enrolment'. This will be considered under option 4. Before leaving option 3, however, it should be noted that if *all* schools 'opted out' of LEA control by seeking grant maintained status, then we would have something very like option 3, with the problems described above.

Option 4 — A System where Schools — State and Private — are all in Competition with each Other

At present only about 7 per cent of pupils are in private schools. But since 1979 Conservative policy has been to encourage the private sector to expand and to blur the distinction between state and private by the government subsidizing or paying for 'bright' pupils transferring to certain private schools (the Assisted Places Scheme introduced under the 1980 Education Act). The operation of APS in terms of giving additional choice has been criticized by Edwards *et al* (1989). It is difficult for a government to promote such a scheme without indicating lack of confidence in the existing state system, especially comprehensive schools.

A distinction also needs to be made between the desirability of having private schools in order to prevent a state monopoly of education, and those who want to maintain independent schools in order to bolster existing social privileges. Crick (1987) has neatly drawn attention to this:

> The argument. . .that the existence of private education is the absolute test case of freedom, would be more impressive if the private schools were not so brazen in arguing that their education constitutes a good investment. (p. 87)

Competition between private and state schools has been encouraged since 1979, but the assumption is that the private model is superior. If it is thought desirable to introduce variations into the existing system, then it is important that the objectives for the innovation are clear and that existing state schools are not disadvantaged in the process. At the end of this chapter I will also make some recommendations about making competition between state and private schools more fair.

Perhaps the more significant aspect of this option is that state schools would not only be in competition with private schools but also in competition with each other. Some have suggested that a combination of LMS and open enrolment at a time of falling rolls (or even when there are more places than pupils) effectively provides a situation in which all schools are competing for pupils and head teachers will be forced to try to encourage parents to choose their school — a quasi-market.

The proponents of market competition claim that such a system brings about higher standards for a number of reasons: parents will choose good schools and, eventually, bad schools close; even if bad schools do not close, it is claimed that the staff get the message and begin to work harder to improve their school; by choosing a school parents are more involved and committed; parents like choice, and choice should not be confined to those who can afford to pay. In addition, Chubb and Moe (1990) in the USA claim that a major gain is freeing the school from 'local democratic control' which 'inevitably' produces ineffective government. In the UK this claim tends to be expressed somewhat differently, in terms of spending more on the schools themselves and less on LEA bureaucrats. This is, of course, a motive behind LMS, which is a much less contentious issue than quasi-markets.

At this stage it will be useful to be able to introduce empirical evidence to help decide whether the claims of those advocating market forces in education can be justified. Chubb and Moe quote a number of examples in the USA where some steps taken towards quasi-markets have resulted in improved standards, at least in the short term. These are sufficiently impressive to make any unbiased reader think carefully about the merits of giving schools much greater control over their budgets, the hiring and firing of staff, etc. In the UK, LMS was intended to bring about just that kind of greater autonomy, but I suspect that Chubb and Moe would speculate that only by making schools *completely* free of LEA control, will you get the full benefits and improved schools. That will have to remain for the present as speculation, but there is relevant empirical data much closer — in Scotland.

In 1980 the Education Act for England and Wales extended parents' rights to choose schools, but did not go nearly as far in terms of limiting the powers of LEAs and schools to set maximum numbers of pupils as the 1988 Act. In Scotland, however, the parallel 'Parents' Charter' Act in 1981 went much further and made the position in Scotland from 1982 onwards much closer to that for England and Wales after 1988. Adler, Petch and Tweedie (1989) seized upon this as an opportunity, inter alia, to test out some of the claims made for the advantages of greater choice for parents and greater competition for the schools. The results are extremely interesting and relevant, even bearing in mind the considerable differences between Scotland, England and Wales.

Adler *et al* show that there is considerable support for the principle of the right to choose, although the vast majority of parents (about 90 per cent) have continued to prefer their local school. This is in keeping with other studies which show that proximity is probably the most important factor in choosing a school. There were significant geographical differences, however, in the percentage of parents opting to exercise choice — ranging from 2 or 3 per cent in rural areas to 25 per cent in some urban districts. And as parents became better informed, the percentage of 'choosers' continued to increase gradually. Where parents exercised choice, they tended to do so for reasons of safety of access, or the 'quality' of the area rather than for better academic standards or opportunities. Contrary to some predictions, there was no evidence that choosing was confined to middle class parents.

All of these findings support the view that parents ought to be given some choice. To what extent they should be exhorted to choose on the basis of schools' test results is a quite different question (not explored in this research).

So much for the advantages of the 'Parents' Charter'. There were also negative features of the 1981 legislation in Scotland. There was no evidence to support the claim that bright working class children in 'deprived' areas particularly benefited from the new arrangements. And there was no evidence (after only five or six years) that the standards of schools (individually or generally) had improved as a result of competition. Schools that attracted more pupils often found it difficult to cope adequately with the increased numbers. On the other hand, no school had closed as a result of market forces, and those schools that had lost numbers of pupils found it difficult to respond positively to parents' wishes — for example, there was little they could do about making access to the school safer, or improving the attractiveness of a rough area; and, once in decline, it was very difficult for schools to recover. There were signs of increasing inequalities, widening of gaps between schools, and the danger of a 'two-tier system' developing. Those, like McPherson and Willms (1987), who had warned that standards might fall as a result of the market, could find some support in this research, although Adler and his colleagues warn us that more time and more evidence is needed.

From the Scottish LEA point of view there were clear disadvantages. It was more difficult (perhaps impossible) to achieve any kind of balanced intake, socially or academically. There were additional costs involved in sustaining smaller classes in less popular schools, as well as other inefficient use of resources. Although it was possible to grant most parents the school of their choice, there was a growing problem of disappointed choosers, including some who were refused a place in their nearest school.

In the context of another kind of disappointment, i.e., choosing a school only to find it was very over-crowded, the researchers quote Hirsch (1977) on 'the tyranny of small decisions' (parents who chose a popular school not knowing in advance how many others would make the same choice, and thereby reducing the desirability of that choice). What this excellent study illustrates in that choice, although desirable in principle, is not a panacea, and that market competition does not automatically solve problems of school organization or even necessarily raise standards. The issues surrounding choice and planning are much more complex than enthusiastic privatizers would have us believe. Perhaps an imporant point is beginning to emerge: the public want choice, and it is very important that they be given as much opportunity to exercise choice as possible. But that is not to say that choice is the most important factor; and care should be taken before constructing a whole system based on market competition — encouraging 'exit' rather than 'voice'.

> *Option 5 — State and Private Schools Complementing Each Other and Co-operating with each Other (Mixed Economy, Planning)*

This may be difficult to distinguish in practice from option 4 above. It is a matter of emphasis — with a more tangible role for LEAs.

Since 1979 Conservative policy has been not only to encourage the extension of the private sector, but also to create categories of schools which are neither pure private nor pure state: the APS is an example of private schools cooperating by admitting state subsidized pupils; GMS and CTCs are examples of schools which have much more autonomy than LEA controlled schools.

Should the state be even more generous in what it would be willing to subsidize? In Denmark and Holland, for example, it is much easier for minority groups to set up schools and have them maintained by state grants. The disadvantage of loss of social cohesion is considered to be outweighed by parental satisfaction and social justice.

Critics of such developments as CTCs say that this reform is purely cosmetic: a better school is provided for a very small number of inner city pupils, whilst doing nothing to improve the quality of education for the majority. It is argued that the priorities should be to improve the whole system on the assumption that what most parents want is a reasonable standard of education in their local school. If it is thought desirable to introduce variations into the existing state system, it is important that the objectives for the innovation are clear and that the existing schools are not thereby disadvantaged.

A further possibility is that state and private schools could co-exist, competing in some respects and cooperating in others.

Much depends on the extent to which competition will generally be regarded as more appropriate than cooperation in education as a whole. Option 3 envisaged a system where all schools opted out of LEA control. Option 4 envisaged a system where parents not only had the right to choose but were encouraged to do so in order to promote the spirit of competition among schools and to create quasi-markets. Option 5 would apply if only a minority of schools became GMS (and CTCs) and where choice, although available as a right, would not dominate the system: most parents would be content to send their children to the local school. Parents would be encouraged to have regard for schools' examination and National Curriculum results, but would be encouraged to look for other qualities as well.

In such a system the LEA would be concerned to advise parents and to coordinate schools in a planned way. A planned system can continue if there are a minority of schools outside its direct influence, and a minority of parents who want to choose schools or change their minds. A planned system with schools cooperating rather than competing cannot, however, survive if all schools and all parents are encouraged to opt out of the planned system.

Option 6 — Only State Schools Permitted

The arguments against the existence of private schools being available for those who can pay are very powerful. Tawney (1931), for example, felt that this was one of the major problems of social cohesion in England. Those who object to the existence of elite and other private schools tend to do so on moral grounds about social justice as well as for the practical social reason that they have the undesirable effect of dividing society culturally.

Many would agree that if independent schools did not already exist, society would be better off without them, but since there is a long tradition of private education in this country, there would now be practical and political difficulties in abolishing them; the way forward may be to try to find ways of accommodating them within a national system in an integrated way, and to try to minimize or eliminate their undesirable qualities. I will return to this point later.

Towards Consensus

I would like now to refer back to the point made by Barr that we should first decide what education service we want and then proceed to questions about the most efficient (from an economic point of view) way of delivering that education. This distinction may be something of an over-simplification since there could be ideological or moral objections to certain kinds of delivery systems (for example, indoctrination or brain-washing), but in general, the distinction will work well as a way of making progress so long as we can ignore the views of those extreme Libertarians who object to state education for moral as well as practical reasons, and those at the other end of the continuum who object to private education for social or moral reasons.

Let us now return to the first stage proposed by Barr — i.e., what kind of education services society needs and is prepared to pay for, before deciding on the most efficient means of delivering those services. I will avoid the temptation to use this as an excuse to embark upon philosophical and sociological discussions about the aims, purposes or goals of education in our kind of society, and instead move directly into general categories of agreement. In other words, this will be a consensus approach rather than a philosophical analysis.

There is general agreement that:

(i) there should be free compulsory education for all 5 to 16;

(ii) education should not be concerned solely with training for work (although this is important), but should be concerned with general social, moral and intellectual development (DES, *Better Schools*, 1985);

(iii) during this period 5 to 16 there are certain kinds of knowledge and experience which should be available to all (legally defined as a National Curriculum in ERA, 1988), but that within and beyond the National Curriculum, some choices will be appropriate (see (vii) below);

(iv) choice is appropriate to cater for different tastes, abilities and learning styles within the context of a *common curriculum* — a common curriculum is not a uniform curriculum;

(v) as society develops, industrially and technologically, the period of 'common experience' tends to lengthen (despite the need eventually for specialization) — at first a common curriculum for primary schools was uncontroversial, since 1988 a National Curriculum 5 to 16 is established, in 1989/90 discussions were taking place (at the DES, NCC and SEAC) about the need for some common elements for all young people up to age 18 or 19 (for example, NCC *Core Skills*, 1990);

(vi) beyond age 16 education and training should still be subsidized by the state, but there is less agreement, as yet no consensus, of the best method of funding — but there is agreement that both FE and HE should expand, (see x below);

(vii) (i) to (vi) above concentrate on 'common needs', but individual differences are also important: the differences are of two broad kinds — social and personal: *social differences* include some legitimate ethnic and religious traditions of minority groups (but bearing in mind that a key function of education is social solidarity) — thus social class differences are much more dubious in this respect;

personal differences include a child's tastes (within limits), aptitudes and abilities, and styles of learning (in the past, politicians and educationists have concentrated on intelligence as the crucial personal difference, but other characteristics are probably as important, if not more important;

(viii) whether an individual proceeds to full-time education post-16 should depend on personal, not social differences (but all should continue to receive education or training of some kind);

(ix) in recent years it has become increasingly common for education 5 to 16 to be expressed in terms of Rights or Entitlement — this is a recognition of the fact that in our society a child is considered to have 'rights' even if his parents place low priority on education (hence compulsory education 5 to 16) — there is no complete consensus on these rights, but some agreement for example, HMI *Curriculum 5–16* spells out 'areas of experience';

(x) there is agreement that post-16 education and training needs to expand (Farmer and Barrel, 1982), but the most effective way to expand is not necessarily by extending compulsory education.

Given this kind of set of 'educational rights' what would be the best way of providing appropriate education services for *all*, with the further proviso that reasonable choice has now been established as a feature of this desirable system? I think we can now exclude options 1, 2, 3 and 6. We can remove 1–3 because complete privatization as a policy is advocated by only a small minority of the population, and because their ideological position can be seen to be unconvincing for reasons outlined above. We should also exclude option 6 from consideration. In one respect the reason will be the same — we have evidence that the majority of the population, at present, favour the retention of private schools even if they have no intention of using them themselves. There is also an argument for the retention of private schools on grounds of liberty and avoiding state monopoly. But we should always bear in mind the point made by Crick above. In addition, there may also be some practical advantages in retaining private schools. First, it is difficult to take away what some people already have and like; a good deal of energy might be expended and the result could be the loss of some good schools; the second advantage is to preserve a safety valve. If any parent (or child) continues to be dissatisfied, for good or bad reasons, with what the state can provide, then it is useful to be able to have a 'private' alternative — for example, a residential school, a special school for maladjusted children and so on. The only problem is who pays? Or how much? And there may be some circumstances where an LEA *might* wish to subsidize such a choice. Inevitably there will be difficult cases.

With options 4 and 5 remaining we are really discussing a choice between state and private schools competing with each other or state and private schools cooperating, presumably as part of some kind of plan. The major point to be decided is whether education as a service lends itself to market competition or planned cooperation or whether some kind of mixed model can be developed.

Conclusions

I suggest five conclusions:

(i) Choice has undoubtedly been oversold as a means of improving education. The retention of some kinds of choice is important, although there is no good reason why a state system could not provide the vast majority of services needed with a reasonable amount of desirable choice available. Nevertheless, some parents may wish to have non-state schools for other reasons (see (iii) below).

(ii) Our assumption should be that most parents will choose a neighbourhood school — the evidence is that what most parents want is a good school close at hand. But some parents will choose a state school, for good or bad reasons, further away. There will be costs involved, but not very great ones. This will include those parents who will want to choose a denominational school. There is probably a tension here between society's need to promote a common culture and a minority's desire to preserve differences in tradition, such as those of the Roman Catholic Church. It is impossible to ignore tradition which encouraged this in the past, and so long as it is felt desirable for Roman Catholic and Church of England communities to have such schools, it will be difficult to deny the same facility to Muslim parents, for example, who want Islamic schools. But, it will be important to maintain the tension and insist that in all matters other than religion, the National Curriculum is followed and all other standards are maintained, including real supervision by local inspectors or HMI.

(iii) Some parents may, for a variety of reasons, such as tradition, snobbery or tastes of various kinds, wish to pay
for their children to attend a private school. It is a pity
that this tradition is so strong in the UK, even if for only
a small percentage of the population, but, given that
tradition, it would not be desirable to close all such schools
and forbid that kind of choice. But all schools should be
required to follow the National Curriculum and to
maintain the same standards as state schools. (If we have
a National Curriculum it should be truly national and
apply to all schools). HMI should inspect them and
publish reports on them. In addition, measures should
be taken to make private schools as non-exclusive as
possible: no school should be allowed to refuse pupils
on grounds of colour, class or religion, and school char-
ters should be scrutinized to ensure that schools which
were originally established 'for the poor of the parish'
have not at some stage been transformed into havens for
the rich. It would be desirable to bring English private
schools closer to the Danish and Dutch models, thus
giving, in theory, all parents the right of choice.

(iv) Is there a case for the state or LEA paying for or subsidizing some children attending private schools? Let
me begin by looking at some reasonable examples of
need.

First, there may be parents working abroad who
might, for good reason, wish to have their children
attend boarding schools in England. At present there
are insufficient state schools with boarding places to
meet the demand, and already a good deal of public
funds spent on independent schools for the children
of diplomats, British Council staff, army officers etc.
Such a practice might be allowed to continue, but it
should be empirically examined whether the most
economically effective way is to buy places in independent schools (it might be better to extend provision in state schools). Social distinctions between army
officers and other ranks could not be justified under
these arrangements.

Second, there might be good reason to pay for some children to attend, for example, specialized music schools on a residential basis. Once again, such schools should be obliged to follow the principles of the National Curriculum and be inspected to ensure the maintenance of standards.

Third, the existing Assisted Places Scheme should be modified over a period of years (ensuring that present pupils' education is not disrupted). Modification will be necessary because if our first principle ((i) above) is that the state system can provide a satisfactory education for all children, then it does not make sense to make an exception for bright children whose parents prefer an independent school. There may be a better case for changing the APS so that it caters for various kinds of other needs such as orphans, children from one-parent families, children whose mother is chronically ill or others who have a genuine need for the special provisions of a residential school. This would be a constructive modification of APS, much better than perpetuating the existing scheme which suggests that state schools are not good enough for academic children. A modified APS might have the beneficial effect of blurring the distinction between state and independent schooling (beneficial socially, but not necessarily economically).

Fourth, what should happen for those for whom an LEA claims it provides an adequate schooling but whose parents are still dissatisfied? In the USA this kind of situation gives rise to the question 'why should only the rich be able to choose?' A system could be developed whereby all parents who had a genuine reason for objecting to their local state schools could apply to the LEA for some assistance to pay for an alternative. There could be a number of valid reasons, but a procedure would be needed to ensure that this kind of choice was rare and also did not become a middle-class privilege.

(v) Universities and polytechnics might be required to acknowledge the fact that a boy from Eton with high scores at 'A' level is probably less academically gifted than a boy or girl with the same scores from a school where there is a much less favourable teacher-pupil ratio and where other resources are more limited. It would not be difficult to apply a crude formula relating the cost of education to the scores gained at 'A' level and requiring admissions tutors to take account of this. Such a procedure would involve recognizing that examination scores are not measures of absolute ability, but are affected by intensity of teaching and other cost-related factors. Some universities make such judgments on an informal basis, but it would be reasonable to formalize procedures as part of a national system. It might also have a marginal effect on some parents wishing to buy privilege.

I will return to these recommendations about choice in the final chapter, where it will be important to retain the distinction between desirable and undersirable choice, fair and unfair choice and the realization that increasing choice for some may have the unintended consequence of reducing choice for others.

Another point was made in chapter 5 which needs emphasis here: there is a difference between offering *real* choices (i.e., where there is a high chance of meeting those choices) and what I will refer to as '*lottery*' choices (where parents might be encouraged to choose but where there will be a very low chance of satisfaction). It may also be as well to bear in mind that there are *trivial* choices offered, and *spurious* choices (the educational equivalent of different brands of petrol which cost the same and make no difference to the running of a car).

Given the above preference for option 5, there are still some unanswered questions about the blurring of distinctions between state and private schools. As part of any consensus plan it will be necessary to clarify the role of CTCs and grant maintained schools, partly to ensure they offer real choices, partly to avoid a new hierarchy of schools, and partly to clarify their aims and possible functions as part of a new consensus.

Towards a New Consensus?

At the beginnig of the new decade, the public mood is
rapidly shifting. 'Markets', 'enterprise', 'choice' — the
bugle calls of the neo-liberal counter-revolution which
seemed destined to carry all before it in the early 1980s —
no longer stiffen many sinews or summon up much blood.
Even among Conservative Ministers the talk now is of
'citizenship', 'responsibility' and 'stewardship'. In the realm
of policy, private interest still holds sway, but there is
not much doubt that in the realm of feeling and aspiration, the pendulum is swinging back to public concern.
Market failure once again looms larger in the public mind
than government failure, and the erosion of community
seems more alarming than the excesses of collectivism.
(Marquand, 1990)

In chapter 6 I examined the concepts of choice and the market as
applied to education. I argued that it was important to distinguish between kinds of choice not all of which could be regarded
as important or even desirable. Choice has become a fashionable
slogan for the new right, but like many slogans it tends to treat
complex issues in a simplistic way. As for the market, it was by
no means clear that simply allowing market forces to operate
would bring about improvements in the education service. Whilst
the 'free' market could be ruled out, a controlled, carefully regulated market, in the sense of private and state schools operating
side by side might provide the basis for an appropriate consensus

policy. The debate about the precise form of national and local planning is likely to continue, but it would be helpful if the debate could take place within a consensus framework. This chapter will be concerned with outlining such a framework.

In November 1990, some time after Marquand had written the above quotation, Margaret Thatcher was forced to resign as Prime Minister. The main reason appeared to be her intransigent attitude to Europe, but for some months before, there had been signs that the tide was beginning to turn against several other aspects of Thatcherism. New Right social and economic policies in the UK, and elsewhere, were increasingly under critical scrutiny.

After twelve years the Conservative economic prescriptions had still not halted British industrial decline, unemployment was again rising, interest rates were very high, and the recession was hurting the middle classes in a variety of ways. Less was heard of monetarism, and plans to increase public spending were no longer taboo. As for social policies, there had been much disquiet over changes in the National Health Service, it was recognized that much more investment was needed in public transport, and environmental or conservation issues were receiving much publicity. Privatization was no longer regarded as an unqualified success: high salary increases for 'the bosses' were criticized even by the right-wing press. In some spheres there was a return to thinking about planning and controls. John Major appeared to want more efficient public services, even if they cost more, and there was even talk of citizens' rights and the need for a citizens' charter.

As is often the case, changes in education tended to lag behind these trends. The Education Reform Act (1988) was being implemented, but its full effects would still take many years to be evaluated.

The area of greatest adverse publicity about ERA was National Curriculum assessment. The first unreported run of the assessment at Key Stage 1 (7-year-old pupils) took place in May 1991; it was greeted with complaints from parents on behalf of children who, it was claimed, were being tested for three weeks rather than being taught. Teachers complained even more bitterly about the time-consuming bureaucratic arrangements involved. They also asserted, despite the contrary evidence, that the tests revealed no information not already available from teacher assessment. The 1991 annual conferences of the teacher unions were vociferous in their condemnation of the Standard Assessment Tasks (SATs) and in their demand for change. A price was now being paid for the political timetable and the 'top down' implementation: the preparation of assessment materials by NFER had been rushed, teachers were insufficiently consulted and inadequately trained in the new assessment procedures.

There were fewer complaints about other 'reforms' such as grant maintained schools and city technology colleges, but reaction to both was much less positive than had been expected. There was a good deal of dissatisfaction about the arrangements for local management of schools (LMS), not least because many schools felt that they were the victims of under-funding (a favourite joke at the annual conferences was that LMS stood for 'less money for schools'). By the summer of 1991 the press was also beginning to latch on to horror stories about the effects of open enrolment. The idea of parents being able to choose schools was splendid in principle, but in many areas there were now bitter complaints about the failure of the system to deliver choice — even if it was an uncomplicated choice of the local comprehensive school. (The rules of the game made it necessary for non-locals to be treated in a way which was no less favourable than those living in the immediate vicinity.) Gradually the advantages of planning, and the impossibility of meeting all parental choices became apparent. Even if market forces in the form of parental choice were to have greater sway, the advantages of some planning seemed to be accepted. The need for a consensus approach was occasionally suggested, despite some examples of extremism on the right (see p. 81 above). LEAs and the public, as well as the professionals, wanted consensus.

A number of adjustments will undoubtedly have to be made in the 1990s, irrespective of what government is in power. Some effects, however, will be irreversible, and it would be unwise, even if it were possible, to revert to the status quo ante 1988. Some kind of national curriculum will be regarded as necessary; LMS is generally regarded as worth retaining; and there would be little point in returning polytechnics and colleges to the LEAs. Much will depend on how many schools eventually opt out, but it is extremely unlikely that LEAs can survive in their present form. It may be that they will have to seek a role in assisting and serving schools rather than trying to retain their planning and control function. This is still disputed territory, but not necessarily a dispute along party lines: some left wing planners have in the past criticized LEAs as an unnecessary tier (Halsey, 1983); some on the right strongly wish to preserve LEAs partly to counter-balance the tendency to over-centralize (Bogdanor, 1991), partly because they think LEAs are doing a very useful job at the local level (Sams, 1991). The suggestion in John Major's Citizens' Charter that school inspection should be removed from LEA control was particularly criticized.

For the rest of this chapter I will attempt to outline the basis of a consensus position on educational policies. As has been indicated several times throughout this book, consensus on educational policies is highly desirable in the present two-party system. I will suggest that there is sufficient common ground to make consensus possible. Not a return to 1944 consensus, but a new set of proposals for the situation arising out of the ERA (1988). In chapter 8 I will move to a detailed consideration of a consensus agenda.

Consensus is a complex, multifaceted concept which needs to be unpacked. I will outline five levels of analysis, going from the most general to the more specific:

   (i)   Values
  (ii)   Other aspects of common culture
 (iii)   The structure of the education service
 (iv)   Education policies
  (v)   Curriculum

My contention will be that at all five levels the similarities between the parties are more important than the differences if we are to embark upon consensus planning.

Level 1 — Values

Consensus must be based on those shared values and aspirations which are held by the majority of the community irrespective of political allegiance. A good deal of this book has been devoted to the ideological differences between groups, especially decision-makers and politicians. But it is equally important to establish what members of a society agree about. One technique for achieving a greater degree of consensus is to move further in the direction of abstract principles. For example, it would be possible to divide British people (and their politicians) into those who support capital punishment for murder and those who oppose it. On that particular issue we could separate adults ideologically, concentrating on the difference between them and the difficulty of reaching agreement on a policy on the death penalty. We could, however, avoid such a dispute by moving beyond the immediate issue and asking more abstract questions about respect for human life, and the crime involved in taking human life. On that more fundamental issue it is easier to reach agreement and establish consensus. The more detailed the proposal the more difficult it will be to avoid conflict, but for some purposes it is necessary to stress common values and beliefs.

And so it is with education. In earlier chapters I have described the ideological differences between four groups on such matters as curriculum, teaching methods, school organization, choice and the market. To achieve anything like consensus there will be two prerequisites: first, a willingness to concentrate on more fundamental principles rather than details; second, to be prepared to make some concessions for the sake of broader agreement. The resulting set of compromises need not be a bland 'lowest common denominator', but could be a dynamic set of tensions to be resolved in a positive way.

For example, some holding the ideological views I have labelled as comprehensive planners would prefer to abolish all private schools in the cause of planning a better system for all. This is a perfectly respectable principle to hold, but could not at present be the basis of consensus planning. Those holding that view would need to be reminded that in a democracy we should be wary of embarking upon legislation which would not have the support of the population. Many public opinion polls have indicated that a high percentage of adults believe that individuals should have the right to choose private education, although they may also say they would not wish to exercise that choice themselves.

Applying the principle of moving to a more abstract level, we would find that the reason why people feel strongly about state schools and private provision is that they place a high value on the worth of education. For our consensus planning, we should, therefore, start from that kind of values agreement and seek to elaborate on why they consider education so highly, and what they want from education, rather than get involved in arguments about school organization and the provision of education. If at that level there are strong disagreements then some choice may be necessary. In Denmark and Holland, for example, there is an expectation that parents, however rich, will use the state system; but there is no compulsion — all parents have a right to make other arrangements and to be subsidized by the state for the education of their children, even if they decide to set up their own 'private' school. It is then found possible for such state and private schools to co-exist, and also to follow certain common requirements such as a core curriculum.

What I hoped to show in chapters 2 and 3 was that although there are ideological differences between the Conservative and Labour parties, they are not so great as to prevent the achievement of consensus. At the level of ideology there are differences, but at a deeper level of values analysis there is likely to be more agreement. The purpose of this chapter is not to ignore the differences, but to seek common ground.

By the end of chapter 3 we might have come up with a list of differences such as the following:

IDEOLOGICAL PREFERENCE

LABOUR	*CONSERVATIVE*
Planning a system for all	Choice
Collectivism	Individualism
Child-centred methods	Traditional methods

But in each case the difference conceals a commitment to more fundamental values such as quality in education, respect for persons as individuals and as members of groups, the search for excellence. It is also possible to see the differences as a question of emphasis and balance rather than total opposition. Few on the left believe in a system which is planned to such an extent that there is no choice; few on the right believe that planning can be avoided altogether. Similarly, there are important differences of view about collectivist and individualist beliefs, but at a deeper level of analysis it can be seen that the opposition between the individual and society is a false one: society is made up of individuals who only attain real humanity by being members of a social group. The third pair of opposites neatly illustrates the false contrast: good teachers use a variety of methods and approaches (and it may also be interesting to note that the child-centred pedagogy might, in some respects, be expected to be associated with individualism rather than collectivism).

Level 2 — Other Aspects of Common Culture

Some anthropologists, such as Benedict (1934), have written about the differences between societies; others, such as Kluckhohn (1962), have emphasized the essential similarities between all societies. The same is true for groups within any one society. It is possible to divide the society by discussing sub-cultural values and beliefs; but it is equally possible (and sometimes beneficial) to concentrate on the values and beliefs which are held in common by all members of society (or at least by most — there are always deviants).

All (or most) members of our society have fundamental beliefs in democracy, justice (or at least fair play), technology, rationality and morality which are more important than ideological differences. Apart from common values we also share respect for institutions such as Parliament, local government, the incorruptibility of civil servants, the independence of HMI and so on.

If, in the limited field of education, planners and political decision-makers were prepared to aim for consensus rather than to exploit conflict, it is clear that there is plenty of common ground on principles and fundamentals, although complete agreement on every detail will rarely be possible.

The list of principles contained in *Better Schools* (DES, 1985) was an interesting attempt at this kind of consensus. An earlier version (DES, 1981) was criticized for being over-general (White, *et al* 1981) but defended by Skilbeck (1984) as a worthwhile declaration of intent:

Principles (DES, 1985)
  (i)   To help pupils to develop lively, enquiring minds, the ability to question and argue rationally and to apply themselves to tasks and physical skills.
 (ii)   To help pupils to acquire understanding, knowledge and skills relevant to adult life and employment in a fast-changing world.
(iii)   To help pupils to use language and number effectively.
(iv)   To help pupils to develop personal moral values, respect for religious values, and tolerance of other races, religions and ways of life.
 (v)   To help pupils to understand the world in which they live, and the interdependence of individuals, groups and nations.
(vi)   To help pupils to appreciate human achievements and aspirations. (*Better Schools*, DES, 1985)

This is not a very sophisticated kind of analysis but it can serve as a general set of aims from which more specific consensus statements can be derived.

Level 3 — Structure of the Education Service

We have seen that consensus is possible where there are shared values; it is also important to identify consensus structures within the system and to note whatever degree of consensus already exists. If there were total lack of consensus, the education service in a democracy would cease to work, but the structure can change as long as it preserves enough consensus to keep the system going. In 1944 the consensus was based on partnership between the central authority, LEAs and teachers. The 1988 changes have in effect moved the education service away from that consensus base by increasing the power of the DES, decreasing the authority of LEAs, downgrading the professionalism of teachers, whilst enhancing the powers of parents and governors. This has destabilized the system and introduced an element of conflict, but not yet caused the system to break down completely. As I suggested at the beginning of this book, however, so much conflict was generated that we came perilously close to a collapse of the system. Whereas the introduction of a little conflict may be good for a system, too much is certainly dangerous.

I have suggested elsewhere (Lawton, 1989b) that it is misleading to talk of the DES as though it were a unity. I suggested that the DES may more usefully be regarded as a 'tension system' consisting of three groups: the politicians, the bureaucrats and the professionals. It is also possible to analyze the whole education system by using the same three categories. Such an analysis may help us to find a prescription for a new kind of consensus at the level of *structure*.

The first group, the politicians in power, have relations with Opposition politicians, politicians in the local authorities, politicians of their own Party in the House of Commons and the Lords, and also directly or indirectly with parents, teachers and governors. Because of the existence of various pressure groups, the politicians in power have to balance ideological doctrines against popular views on education. This can have the effect of moderating extreme doctrines. But sometimes when politicians have a very large majority they may be tempted to ignore outside pressures. In the 1987/88 discussions of the ERA there was a tendency for Kenneth Baker and his colleagues to ignore much of the advice given. They presumably hoped that feelings were not so strong that they would cause real damage to the operations of the Act.

Politicians also have to maintain relations with bureaucrats and professionals. Civil servants are trained to obey their political masters, but there are limits. Similarly, a wise Secretary of State tries to carry the professionals with him as far as possible. The classic case outside education was the need for Nye Bevan to gain the cooperation of the medical profession when he introduced the National Health Service. Had he failed, the system he proposed would have been unworkable. In 1987/88 Baker made the mistake of not trying harder to take the teaching profession with him when negotiating ERA. I have already pointed out some examples of the difficulties, such as tests for the 7-year-olds, which might have been avoided.

If we regard the whole education service as a three-sided tension system, then quite clearly the least stable of the three is the political. Bureaucrats can be, and are, moved but this can only be done in moderation; teachers and their professional organizations are much more stable than politicians who face re-election every five years and possible reshuffles more frequently. But, in passing, we should also note that the professionals as represented by the teachers' unions are, in England and Wales, notoriously lacking in unity — there are too many unions frequently fighting among themselves to be as powerful as they could be.

One analysis of the period 1979–88 would be to show that the politicians and the bureaucrats were pursuing similar (but not identical) goals — especially in terms of more central control of the system — at a time when the professionals were weakened and demoralized by the failure of the programme of teacher action in the mid-1980s.

Conflict prevailed because the politicians and bureaucrats together could easily defeat the professionals. Consensus and partnership were no longer seen as high priority. But this was a dangerous game to play: sooner or later the teachers had to be persuaded to operate the new system. Coercion was not a realistic long-term option. Eventually a move back towards consensus is desirable, if not essential.

There is another aspect of consensus which should be discussed at this level. The 1944 consensus rested on the notion of partnership. Partnership between the central authority in education, LEAs and the teachers. This partnership has been threatened during the 1980s: the power of the DES, parents and governors has been increased, but the powers of the LEAs have been reduced and teacher professional autonomy threatened. If we relate that change to the tension system, we see that politicians and bureaucrats have gained power at the expense of the professionals (not just teachers, but also HMI and LEA experts). The 1944 version of partnership was obsolescent by the 1980s: giving too little control to the DES, too much to LEAs, and the wrong pattern of autonomy to schools. But great care should be taken before abolishing the whole of that basis for consensus. Part of the move back to consensus ought to involve a search for a new kind of partnership within the tension system, since it is most unlikely that the 1944 partnership model can ever be revived.

LEAs will be permanently weakened, and even the future of HMI is being questioned (by both political parties). A new consensus ought to be seeking means of strengthening the professionals without giving them too much power. One possibility would be a General Teaching Council (GTC) giving the profession itself control over admissions, qualifications and discipline, as is the case in Scotland.

Several strategies for a new consensus might work: there is no one magic formula. What I would wish to emphasize, however, is the need to have regard for the tension system and the need to develop a new model of partnership. Crucial to the specific strategy will be the future of LEAs: it is not yet clear how they will emerge from the combined effects of CTCs, GMS, LMS and losing HE, FE and sixth-form colleges. But it is unlikely that a system could work which consisted of a very strong central authority in direct control of thousands of school governing bodies.

Consensus has to be based not only on shared values and common culture, but on an agreed structure or system. Part of the 1944 consensus was the idea of partnership — never carefully defined at the time, but reasonably well understood by those involved. It was a structure described as a national system locally administered. In theory the Minister of Education (later the Secretary of State) had considerable powers, but in practice it was understood that these powers were executed locally by the LEAs, and often by the schools themselves.

By the 1980s this structure was showing signs of strain: Aldrich and Leighton (1985) called for a new Act, and even without the events of 1979–91, there would have been some necessary adjustments, not least in the field of curriculum. Another disadvantage of the partnership with LEAs was the wide divergence of performance by LEAs: some were much more generous than others; some were more efficient. This resulted in gross inequalities between children in the best and the worst LEAs. Sooner or later the Labour Party would have been concerned to reduce those differences, and it would not have been possible without reducing the powers of LEAs. It had often been suggested that in reality there was no *national* system because there were so many differences in standards and patterns of organization throughout the country. The Labour Party would probably have tackled the problem very differently from the Conservative policies 1979–91, but the result would still have been a change in the relationship between the three partners: the DES, the LEAs and the teachers in the schools. LEAs needed to relinquish or share some of their acquired responsibilities, but it would be disastrous if they were now so damaged that they ceased to function effectively in any way.

The Conservative Party seems to have mixed feelings about LEAs. They usually reaffirm the need for LEAs, but occasionally treat them with contempt. In reconstructing a new consensus partnership, two points need to be borne in mind: the first is the principle of 'subsidiarity' (i.e., that power of control should be delegated down to the most efficient level); the second the related fact that our EEC colleagues are cautiously moving in the direction of devolving more powers to local authorities. It is already becoming apparent in 1991 that there are dangers in neglecting LEAs and giving too much control to schools themselves. LEAs will be needed to ensure minimum standards and to develop local policies on such matters as children with special needs. A national system would ideally have national standards not vast differences between individual schools. This remains a problem to be solved.

Level 4 — Policies

There is already a good deal of agreement about many aspects of education policy. The vast majority of the population (but not quite all) accept the need for a compulsory period of school attendance. We have compulsion for a slightly longer time than many other societies (5–16), but ironically our national achievement in educating a wider age range — say 3–18 — is poor compared with the participation rate and qualifications achieved elsewhere. For example, most Western European countries have more extensive participation for the 3–5 age group and for the 16–18 group. This might suggest that our way forward is not to propose an extension of compulsion, but to improve the quality of the provision — that is improving the opportunities in terms of places available as well as in the quality of the service. To increase compulsion might be an unnecessary threat to consensus, and is not necessarily the most effective means of making progress.

It may be useful at this point in the argument to look at the question of education reform stage by stage, to see how much was achieved by the ERA (1988) and during the years 1988–91 and to see how much remains to be done as part of a new consensus approach.

Early Years

Schooling in England and Wales begins at age 5 and even a little before if a space is available. This compulsory early start used to be regarded as one of the advantages of the English system, but in recent years many societies have made better provision for children in the 'early years' (i.e., from age 3 to 6) because they provide, without compulsory attendance, places for a much higher percentage of this age group than is available in the UK. This problem was, however, untouched by the ERA and should become part of the consensus agenda.

Primary Schools

At their best, English primary schools have served as a model for many other societies. *At their best*, they were — and are — superb; but a succession of reports by Her Majesty's Inspectorate (HMI) and other evidence in the 1970s and 1980s highlighted a number of problems. One defect was that certain areas of knowledge and experience seemed to be neglected, including science, history and geography. Another complaint was that some very able children were not given sufficient opportunity to make progress, whilst those with special needs did not always receive the help they required. In the popular press and in some political documents 'progressive methods' were alleged to be the cause of these ills, but the evidence provided a much more complex picture. The fact that many parents send their children to state primary schools but use private secondary schools, must indicate a higher degree of satisfaction at the primary stage, although there is sometimes a suspicion of a lack of 'stretching' for more able primary pupils.

Secondary Schools 11–16

One of the undesirable features which has existed for many years is that secondary schools are 'examination-driven' and dominated by the demands of higher education (HE). By the mid-1980s the secondary examination structure had evolved into a three-tier system for 16 year old pupils: General Certificate of Education Ordinary level (GCE 'O' level) for the most 'academic' 20 per cent of the population; the Certificate of Secondary Education (CSE) for the next 40 per cent or so; and no school leaving examination or qualification for the supposed 'bottom 40 per cent' of the ability range. A system which 'failed' more than one third of its young people was — apart from any question of social justice — clearly inadequate for a society in which unskilled and semi-skilled jobs were in rapid decline. This deficiency was partly corrected by the establishment of GCSE in 1988 for all pupils, but a legacy of a 'culture of failure' remains in many secondary schools. No society has completely solved the problem of catering for less academic adolescents in a system of compulsory schooling, but the English pattern was, and is, particularly bad in this respect.

Another feature of this inadequacy was the lack of a broad and balanced curriculum for many young people. HMI and others criticized many schools for lack of adequate curriculum planning, and for the 'options systems' which often resulted in boys and girls giving up important subjects at age 14. We had a secondary system with a national examination structure but no agreed curriculum; it was a system which offered little or nothing to a large percentage of young people. It was a failure system rather than a system based on successful progression. This problem has only been partly solved by the introduction of a National Curriculum.

A related and much discussed weakness of English secondary

schools was a much more deep-rooted cultural problem: Corelli Barnett (1986) and Martin Wiener (1985) had both, in different ways, suggested that our education system had, since the nineteenth century been hostile towards the industrialized culture which had developed, and had failed at all levels to encourage young people to participate in it. This problem also remains although it has been tackled to some extent by such initiatives as TVEI and by the technology provisions of the national curriculum. Much remains to be done as was acknowledged by John Major's speech 3 July 1991 (see chapter 5).

16 to 19

There are a number of outstanding problems here, some of them continuations of the 11–16 issues outlined above, including the fact that about half of young people leave school at 16, many of them destined to receive *no* further education or training.

The two other main problems, addressed in the White Paper 1991 but by no means solved, are first the unsatisfactory 'A' level structure, and second, its isolation from other courses 16–19. The weight of opinion was that the White Paper was destined to failure because it did not deal adequately with those two problems.

Higher Education, Including Teacher Education

Once again the main problem is the question of widening access: too few of our young people enter HE; once they are there, the system works extremely well for them (fewer than 14 per cent fail or drop out). But not enough get into HE, and this creates problems of scarcity of skilled personnel, including a shortage of those eligible to enter teaching. This problem was not included in the ERA (1988) which concentrated on the question of *control* of HE; the White Paper in HE (1991) has made some progress (see discussion in chapter 5), but a good deal remains to be achieved.

Level 5 — Curriculum

In the past (Lawton, 1973 and 1989a) I have tried to develop a consensus view of education and the curriculum by means of a cultural analysis approach. I will not repeat the cultural analysis argument here. Instead, I will start by making an assumption about curriculum and education, which is probably uncontroversial, and then proceed to more detailed analysis.

The uncontroversial assumption I want to make is that culture serves to bind a society together. Without culture there can be no society. The definitions of both words involve circular arguments: no society without culture; no culture without society. The purpose of any education system is to ensure that culture is transmitted to the next generation. (Even the word 'transmitted', however, may be an impediment to consensus: let me hasten to say that my use of the word does not imply a one-way communication to passive students; 'transmitted' is a useful shorthand term but I willingly accept that the young do not simply 'receive' culture — all education is necessarily a dynamic process, and students in receiving culture will inevitably transform it.)

Education is therefore concerned with offering the young whatever is so highly regarded that most people believe it would be essential for anyone growing up and participating in their society. We can come back to curricular details in chapter 8. There is now broad agreement between the parties on the need for a National Curriculum (the Labour Party's main complaint about the National Curriculum as included in the ERA (1988) was that the Labour Party had thought of it first). There is not even much dispute about the detailed content of the National Curriculum. My suggestions in chapter 8 will include the recommendation that we should build on that agreement, resist any temptation to embark on a massive replanning of the National Curriculum and assessment programme, but do everything to win the teachers over to what is proposed, including removal of some of the detailed prescriptions.

Agenda for a New Consensus

The idea of a learning society offers a broad vision. It rejects privilege — the idea that it is right for birth to determine destiny. It transcends the principle of meritocracy, which selects for advancement only those judged worthy and rejects as failures those who are not. A learning society would be one in which everyone participated in education and training (formal or informal) throughout their life. It would be a society characterized by high standards and low failure-rates. (Sir Christopher Ball, (1991, p. 12)

In chapter 7 I looked briefly at the basis for consensus which already exists in the present system. I also looked at some of the problems of the education service and asked to what extent they had been solved by the ERA (1988) and the events 1988–1991. Five levels of consensus were analyzed: the broad agreement that exists on questions of *values*; on other aspects of common *culture*; on the *structure* of the education system; and on the more specific questions of education *policy* and *curriculum*. In this final chapter I want to move from that more general discussion to a programme or agenda for consensus in education, on the assumption that similar problems will need to be tackled whatever party is in power, and that a consensus approach would be more productive than a continuation of conflict.

One of the purposes of studying the history of the Labour and Conservative Parties' education policies was to show that neither party has developed a satisfactory vision for education. The 1944 Act was a consensus approach which was part of a desire for a better, fairer society after World War 2. As a consensus programme it was incomplete and was, for a variety of reasons, never achieved, although much was gained in the years after the war.

The period 1944–1979 was spent in modifying the 1944 consensus, being distracted from some of its intentions, even going back on some major decisions. Part of the reason for this lack of direction was the absence of anything as powerful as the 1944 settlement; education became an area of drift rather than direction.

From 1979, however, a new Conservative vision of a kind began to emerge. But it was not a consensus vision. It was an impoverished vision which was also socially divisive and potentially destructive. It was impoverished because it focused mainly on the relation between school and work, and saw the link between schools and the community largely in terms of parental choice. It was potentially destructive because it destabilized the delicate partnership structure without putting anything adequate in its place.

Despite these shortcomings the Conservatives did take a number of steps in the direction of reform: for example, establishing a National Curriculum, looking for a new structure 16–19, and proposing a unified system of higher education. Yet all of these reforms were distorted by a lack of real feeling for the needs of a national education service. Despite some rhetoric to the contrary, the Conservatives still tended to see a separated system, with what was provided for the majority being inferior to what they wanted for their own children. The 1988 Education Act, unlike the 1944 Act, was introduced in a spirit of conflict, with a demoralized and defeated teaching profession in the background.

What then could provide us with a consensus vision of education based on the shared values and common culture discussed in chapter 7? The answer is not original, nor is it utopian. Many educationists, especially those associated with the development of education on an international scale, such as OECD, UNESCO and the Council of Europe, have presented programmes with such titles as 'Permanent Education', 'Life-long Education' and 'Recurrent Education'. More recently, Christopher Ball (1991) has used the expression 'the learning society'.

The motives behind such programmes have combined universalist ideals and answers to practical questions. The ideals were straightforward: that we should think of education not in terms of a compulsory period 5–16, but as a life-long process — from the cradle to the grave. Second, that we should think about education in that way for *all* members of society — not education for a minority and basic training for the rest. So much for the ideal; the more practical reason for looking at education in a new way was the search for more realistic alternatives to the demand for longer and longer periods of uninterrupted, full-time education and training for more and more young people. The solution has been to break down long courses of education or training into units or modules which could be taken separately, full-time or part-time, over longer periods of time. In England the Open University provided one useful model, and, more recently, the National Council for Vocational Qualifications (NCVQ) has been given the task of providing for large numbers in the 16–20 age group.

The key to progress is to see practical solutions not in isolation but as part of the whole picture of a reformed education service. Back to the vision of education as a life-long entitlement for all, not only concerned with improving work skills (although these are very important) but with improving the general quality of life for individuals and the whole community.

From that kind of vision we have to proceed to more detailed aims, and also to some kind of delivery system. The trouble with the Conservative reforms since 1979 was that they were based on a view of a divided society with a divided education system. It was a fatal flaw. Although other industrial societies have problems of implementing education reform, few have the problem of a society as divided as ours. The first task of any genuine reform will be to move away from that kind of segregation to the kind of vision described by Christopher Ball in the quotation which heads this chapter.

In this chapter I want to go on from that kind of vision to a discussion of those policies which should be embraced by any administration seeking consensus. By the 1980s the time was ripe for some degree of greater centralization, but the process has almost certainly gone too far (at just the time when other highly centralized systems such as France and Sweden were moving in the opposite direction). Local authorities must be given a clear — if diminished — role in the new system; and teachers' professional autonomy must be enhanced. Without those two prerequisites, the details that follow are unlikely to succeed.

The New Structure: LEAs

A new role for LEAs is closely connected with the whole question of choice and school autonomy which was discused in chapter 7. A consensus policy for LEAs should be based on a number of interrelated factors. First, despite teething problems, it is clear that LMS policies are here to stay: there is little, if any, difference between the parties on the benefits of the increase in autonomy gained by schools from the budgetary control and personnel matters transferred from LEAs. There is a difference between the parties on GMS, but maybe not an insurmountable one. The Labour Party has threatened to return all grant maintained schools to LEA control; but others have suggested the alternative policy of recommending that all schools should seek and be granted grant maintained status (Halsey made a similar proposal in 1983). In any case, if all schools have almost total control over their budget there may be little difference between LEA schools with LMS and those schools with grant maintained status. The real point will be that LEAs will certainly be left with greatly reduced power and control and should be rethinking their new position very carefully. They will need to become much more like advisory bodies providing services than authorities with control over details of school organization and administration.

There is much to be said in favour of the continued existence of LEAs, even if some of their services will have to be offered on a subscription or fee paying basis rather than on the present compulsory system. LEAs would retain a number of important statutory responsibilities, but be less directly involved in the organization and management of schools. The education service would no longer be a national system locally administered by LEAs, but a national system administered largely by the schools themselves, but with various standards monitored by LEAs. We should, therefore, think of LEA tasks in two categories: those which they would be obliged to carry out, and those which they could offer (in competition with other agencies) on a fee paying basis. There might well be some debate about some services in the grey areas. The following is one possible structure:

(i) LEA statutory responsibilities:
    (a) to coordinate choice of schools and pre-school provision and offer information services to parents;
    (b) to deal with appeals from parents if they fail to get their first choice of school;
    (c) to coordinate information to parents on examinations and test results;
    (d) inspection of schools and pre-school services to ensure minimum standards and to report results to the DES;
    (e) responsibility for the delivery of National Curriculum assessment and processing results;
    (f) to monitor health and safety regulations in all schools;
    (g) to liaise with, and be responsible for the inspection of, private schools within the LEA;
    (h) to have overall responsibility for children with special educational needs. (SEN pupils would carry a 'premium', i.e., schools would be paid more per capita for for such pupils according to the severity of their special needs; LEAs would be responsible for classifying such children and for ensuring that the services provided by schools were adequate);
    (i) to offer INSET, and advice about courses, especially on National Curriculum. (This is a possible 'grey area' which might be optional rather than compulsory);
    (j) to coordinate adult education services.
(ii) Optional services to be offered on a fee or subscription basis:

(a) to offer the services of the LEA psychologists;
(b) to offer advisory services of a subject or phase kind;
(c) to provide personnel expertise;
(d) to provide legal advice.

The New Structure: Schools

Closely related to changes in LEA functions will be the changed status of schools. A number of studies have connected improvements in academic standards with increased autonomy of the schools. Once again, there is no serious party political difference on this: both have supported the idea of school autonomy with enhanced teacher professionalism. In the past there has been a tendency for Conservative politicians to stress the importance of school autonomy in order to promote greater competition between schools, and this aspect of LMS and open enrolment has, it was suggested in chapters 6 and 7, been over-sold. The real advantage of autonomy is not to compete with other schools but to improve the quality of education within the school. This is still an area of dispute but one where the parties are tending to converge.

Studies of effective schools have listed the characteristics associated with school effectivenesss, but generally do not offer much advice on how to acquire such characteristics. Others have pointed out that the prerequisites for school effectiveness are extremely similar to the characteristics of those schools successful in the processes of self-evaluation, school-based curriculum development and school-based staff development. They approach the problem of improvement from different angles but end up with very similar scenarios. For example, Purkey and Smith (1983) in a review of the vast school effectiveness literature identified nine characteristics:

(i) Adequate autonomy for Principal and staff to devise their own paths to improvement.
(ii) Educational leadership.
(iii) Staff stability.

    (iv)   Good curriculum planning and implementation.
    (v)   Staff development/INSET.
    (vi)   Parental involvement and support.
    (vii)   Public recognition of academic success within the school.
    (viii)   Maximized learning time (time on task).
    (ix)   Local authority support.

They stressed, however, that the crucial characteristic of effective schools was that the above features were part of a distinctive school culture. It would not be possible to achieve effectiveness simply by tackling the characteristics one by one. Similar results have been found in British studies such as Rutter *et al* (1979) and Mortimore *et al* (1989). One of the most important features of all these studies is the emphasis on school autonomy, professionalism and team work as part of the school culture. In this respect there is still much to be done in England and Wales to put right the damage of recent years when teachers' perceptions of their own status has been that their autonomy has diminished and their prestige has declined.

The New Structure: The Teaching Profession

Whatever the precise form of a consensus programme for schools, it is very likely that greater demands will be made on the teachers. To some extent this has already happened: the National Curriculum, and especially the assessment of pupils, has increased the responsibilities of teachers who will be required to provide detailed information for parents about their children's levels of attainment. But the morale of teachers is low, and their status, salaries and conditions of service have not kept pace with similar groups.

    There has been a good deal of discussion about the need to change public attitudes towards education — a change in the culture — and a key part of this change must be to raise the esteem of the teaching profession. An important insight into the difficulty of this change was provided by the work of Linda Darling-Hammond and her colleagues (1983) in the USA, who focused on 'conceptions of teacher work'. They suggested that four very different conceptions existed in the minds of politicians, administrators and the general public: teaching as routine labour, teaching as a craft, teaching as a professional activity, or teaching as an art. In the UK in recent years there has been a lack of consistency in the way in which teachers have been treated by politicians: on the one hand, they are denied professional conditions and on occasion are dictated to rather than consulted; on the other hand, the National Curriculum and assessment are put forward in the context of adding to teachers' professional responsibilities. One key factor is that appraisal has been forced upon the profession, as a condition for a salary award, in a way which reinforces the image of teachers as routine workers whose achievements need to be carefully checked on a regular basis. Professional appraisal, however, should emphasize professional development and in-service education rather than being conducted in the context of the threat of dismissal or the possibility of promotion.

A simple way of enhancing the prestige of teachers would be to give them greater control over the registration of new entrants to the profession, including the specification of qualifications and training required. Some politicians fear that a General Teaching Council, such as already exists in Scotland, would be dominated by the teachers' unions. Such an outcome is not inevitable: the General Medical Council is kept quite separate from the BMA, and safeguards (as well as adequate representation of employers) could be built-in to a structure for a GTC. The case for a GTC has long been advocated by a number of professional groups (Sayer, 1985).

Perhaps even more important than a GTC is a new approach to teacher education and training. Changes are needed partly for reasons of professional status, partly because the existing system is in danger of breakdown and failing to deliver the number of good quality teachers required.

During the 1990s there will be a fall in the number of school leavers, and a shortage of (or at least a greater demand for) graduates. In other words, there will be much greater competition for 'teacher material' than in previous years. This will provide a classic situation of increasing demand and diminishing supply which would — in a free market — lead to much higher salaries. But of course the market is not free; it is to some extent controlled by the DES. Meanwhile there are other important factors in the supply-demand relationship which complicate the formula (and almost certainly aggravate the recruitment problem).

One of the features of teacher supply is that it is heavily, and increasingly, dependent on females: in 1986/87 of the overall under-25 intake only 21 per cent were male (32 per cent of secondary; only 9 per cent of primary). But during the 1990s other employers hungry for graduates will almost certainly be trying to attract such young women into a variety of other graduate level occupations where the salary structure and conditions of service may well be more attractive than teaching.

A further difficulty: in 1986/87 of the 14,500 female teachers recruited to primary schools, only about one-third were new entrants to the profession; approximately two-thirds were 're-entries' — i.e., women who had temporarily interrupted their career for child-rearing or other reasons. When questioned about teacher supply, DES politicians tend to make much of the fact that there are so many such trained teachers in the PIT (the 'pool of inactive teachers'). But they are, of course, a rather unpredictable group, comparatively immobile, and open to other offers of employment — or no employment at all, if they so choose. Add to that the evidence provided by Professor Smithers (1990) about the increasing rate of wastage in the profession, and we have a picture of teacher supply during the 1990s which could become disastrous — unless appropriate action is taken.

It may not just be difficult to recruit enough teachers during the 1990s — it may be impossible, if traditional routes are relied upon. Pressures to recruit more and more unqualified teachers or under-qualified licensed teachers will be enormous. It will be difficult for the teacher unions to resist pressures to employ the unqualified or under-qualified. A better strategy for them might be to welcome such recruits as teacher assistants and to concentrate on proper professional standards for those reaching full professional teacher status, and to delineate carefully the professional aspects of the teacher's role from the others.

Teaching is already a difficult and demanding job, and in the 1990s it will become more so, not least as a result of the National Curriculum and its assessment. The solution will be to have a more stratified teaching force where only the best qualified are regarded as professional teachers.

Teacher education will need to be very different from the kind of programme common in the 1980s. Initial teacher education will concentrate on shorter, more intensive courses, involving preparation for the classroom. More of this training — but not all — will be school-based. There will still be a place for preparation for the next forty years rather than the immediate requirements of the classroom. During the second stage, induction/probation, the emphasis will change, encouraging teachers to reflect about practice as well as to become better practitioners. The third stage will concentrate on professional concerns: encouraging teachers to understand the curriculum as a whole, for example, and to reflect on teaching with reference, when appropriate, to the potential contributions of such disciplines as philosophy, psychology and sociology. But that will not be the end of the story. Professional teachers will need opportunities for continuous education, not only to update their skills and rethink their methods, but to develop as human beings and professional teachers in a variety of ways. Part-time research into the processes of teaching and learning should be a high priority for them. Any government should immediately begin to negotiate shorter programmes for initial training with the guarantee of fully professional arrangements for induction and INSET over the whole period of a teaching career. This kind of new deal for teachers, together with the General Teaching Council, would produce dramatic results in a comparatively short period of time.

An Agenda for Consensus — with Targets

Within that broad framework of a reformed structure, it may now be useful to look at the proposed new consensus policies stage by stage — that is from pre-school provision to higher education and beyond.

Early Years

The inadequate provision of education for the 3 to 5 age group remains. Part of the problem is that responsibility for this age group is currently shared between the DES and DHSS which is concerned with 'nursery provision'. It has yet to be accepted by the government that the need of this age group is education rather than child care.

The *target* for a new government should be the provision of some kind of educational service for all who want it by the end of the decade. The policy should be not to extend compulsion, but to encourage a variety of provision from part-time playgroups to full-time nursery schools according to choice. Patricia Hewitt (1989) made the interesting suggestion that such pre-school provision could best be provided by a voucher system: the vouchers could be spent on any approved kind of pre-school service according to need or choice.

This is an interesting consensus development. Vouchers have in the past been associated with the right-wing of the Conservative Party, but in this case they are being put forward as a solution to a problem by someone at the centre of the Labour Party. There is, of course, no real reason why vouchers at this stage or any other should be regarded as right-wing: vouchers can be adapted, as Jencks (1970) in the USA suggested, in a redistributive way, and in this case the vouchers could be adjusted according to income, or, as Le Grand (1990) suggests, according to district — creating some kind of positively discriminatory voucher (PDV).

The government's main responsibility would be to make sure that provision for all of some kind must be available, with standards being monitored by LEAs.

Primary Schools

Some improvements may be achieved, in time, by the National Curriculum and its assessment, despite the shortcomings mentioned above. But we know that many primary schools are inadequately housed and equipped (see the annual reports of Her Majesty's Senior Chief Inspector). Another problem for primary schools is the growing shortage of qualified teachers.

A realistic *target* will be to eliminate sub-standard accommodation by the end of the decade; and by that time to have eradicated non-reading by the age of 11, to improve the teaching of mathematics, science and technology; in order to achieve all that, adequate INSET for all primary teachers will be essential.

Secondary Schools

The National Curriculum may help to improve secondary schools but will not in itself solve the problem of the 'culture of failure' already referred to. Before the comprehensive system was introduced, the major difference between grammar schools and secondary modern schools was that grammar schools tended to be where pupils succeeded and secondary modern schools were institutions characterized by failure. An unintended consequence of the comprehensive system was that comprehensive schools often tended to inherit some of the culture of failure from the secondary moderns. Failure is a dominant characteristic of the secondary school system in other respects.

The *target* for secondary schooling can be expressed in terms of performance at 16. There is a consensus that a much higher percentage of school-leavers should have reached the kind of levels of achievement at present attained by a minority. There must be a move away from dominance of the curriculum by GCSE (although GCSE will remain for some years as the publicly accepted set of standards); the main advantage of the TGAT model of ten levels of achievement is, however, that it should be used to encourage high achievers to reach GCSE standards, or their National Curriculum equivalent levels 7 to 10, whenever they are ready, rather than waiting for the month of June in their sixteenth year. The TGAT levels of achievement should be used in the same way as graded assessment examinations — i.e., students reach a level when they are ready and are given the appropriate tests by their teacher (externally moderated). This reform should be accompanied by a more flexible teaching style: one of the lessons learned by teachers from TVEI was that students reach much higher standards when learning is experiential and students work in a way which is more problem-centred and resource-based. Conservative politicians have consistently stressed that the

National Curriculum is a guide not a strait-jacket. The individual needs and interests of students should be given priority by teachers, within the guidelines of the National Curriculum, and bearing in mind raising standards. By 1999 a realistic target would be that 80 per cent of the population should reach levels 7 to 10 in English, maths and science and at least two other subjects. (The Labour Party has already fixed on a target of 80 per cent reaching GCSE Grades A to C in five subjects.) But it will be important for secondary schools to go beyond national curriculum subjects and to give priority to some cross-curricular areas such as health education and personal and social development (including education for citizenship of an enlightened kind). It will be necessary to establish suitable targets for those areas as well — the National Curriculum Council is likely to make suggestions on this.

16 to 19

That brings us to the other major area of muddle and confusion untouched by the ERA (1988).

We have seen that the problems 16–19 may be summarized as:

(i)   too few remaining in the system; about half receiving no educational training after 16;

(ii) the dominant course 16–19 is GCE A Level which has for many years been regarded as too narrow, too specialized and over-academic in content and methods;

(iii) there are unnecessary barriers between academic 'A' level courses and the more vocationally oriented programmes such as BTEC.

I have spent some time on education and training 16–18 in earlier chapters partly because it is a longstanding cultural problem of English education, and partly because it illustrates very clearly the need for consensus. It is a good example of broad agreement between the parties on principles and fundamentals, but much less agreement at the level of detailed policy. As time passes, the various proposals coming from the Labour Party and the Conservative Party get closer together. But it will eventually be necessary to say that there can be no solution that will satisfy everyone on every detail. A consensus solution will require a willingness to compromise as well as the avoidance of entrenched ideological details and slogans such as 'retaining the gold standard' which not only oversimplify the problem, but also serve to prevent rational discussion of it.

In this particular case there may be external pressure from Europe after 1992 which may help to resolve the problem. 'A' levels have survived so long because they enable universities to offer three-year degrees in most subjects. But that uniformity is already breaking down. The pressure to harmonize with Europe and to have our professional qualifications accepted by other European countries may push us towards longer degree programmes in some subjects, such as engineering, hence relieving the pressure on 18 year olds to have covered some 'university ground' during their 'A' level courses. This might be the most important factor in the debate, and has been anticipated to some extent by university Vice-Chancellors in their discussions of a broader curriculum 16–18.

Target: at present fewer than 20 per cent of 18-year-olds achieve anything like the standard of NVQ Level 3 — such as BTEC National or two 'A' levels. Both Parties are committed to greatly improved standards of achievement (although at present they differ on the means). Ball (1991) recommended 60 per cent of the age group reaching that broadly defined level. This should be achievable by 1999 provided that the 'A' level system is replaced by a more flexible and coherent structure (whilst preserving standards). But it will not be achievable if 'A' levels continue in isolation. An additional target should be for *all* young people to continue in education and training on a part-time basis at least until the age of 18.

Finance may be a problem, but this should not be allowed to delay progress to the above targets. This is another area where vouchers might provide a suitable means. Experiments in a few areas are already in progress, and the opportunity should be taken to evaluate these experiments and to learn from them.

Higher Education

The main aim must be to expand numbers and to improve opportunity for access for working class students. Le Grand (1990), and several others, have accepted the idea of quasi markets in this field and suggest that vouchers could help simplify the funding problem. Universities should charge full fees to students who would be given vouchers to cover tuition fees and basic maintenance, thus cutting out the need for the UFC or its successor to allocate places and grants to universities — instead a quasi market would operate. The Funding Council would only need to allocate money for research. Vouchers for students could be supplemented by loans, and for the sake of equity, a graduate tax (payable by means of national insurance contributions) could recoup some of the money later. Without such a financial mechanism it is unlikely that any Party would think they could afford to expand higher education on the scale that is now required. Given that financial arrangement, however, there is no reason why by the end of the decade a *target* participation rate of 40 per cent should not be achieved.

Teacher Education

The Council for the Accreditation of Teacher Education (CATE) has established national standards for initial teacher education, and hence, indirectly, standards for entry into the profession. Although some of these 'criteria' were more controversial than others, most educationists would accept the desirability of having some national guidelines for courses which carry qualified teacher status, and most would accept the desirability of raising standards for entry into the teaching profession. But it is inconsistent that at precisely the same time, we have had pressures from the political right to abandon all such controls and restrictions, even to abandon teacher training altogether (Hillgate Group, 1989; O'Hear, 1988; Cox, 1989). The compromise achieved during the late eighties was to retain teacher training, with higher standards, and at the same time to introduce new routes into the profession, such as licensed teachers and articled teachers where the emphasis is placed on training within the school rather than in institutions of higher education. I suggest that this kind of inconsistency cannot continue indefinitely, even on grounds of equity, and that some kind of rationalization of qualified teacher status will be essential to avoid the collapse of the traditional system.

The major conflict will be the need for greater professionalism and the inability to pay (or unwillingness to pay) for a larger, highly paid teaching force. A radical solution will be called for — namely a more hierarchical profession reflecting different levels of qualification, training and experience.

The implications of such changes for teacher education are quite clear and are in line with other aspects of professional development. ITT should be regarded as the first stage of initiation into the profession of teaching rather than a licence to practise for the next forty years. ITT would then concentrate more on practical classroom skills and techniques and would not even pretend to provide a basis for the rest of a professional career. This would not mean, of course, that the traditional educational disciplines cease to possess any relevance — simply that they would perform a different function at a later professional stage. All this would reinforce some of the arguments of the James Report (DES, 1972b) which suggested that ITT should be followed by an induction period, and that later in their career all teachers should have the right to further professional study on a full-time basis.

There should be a three-stage process of professionalization: initial training/licensing; followed by a period of probation/induction which would include further study before obtaining qualified teacher status; finally, after further courses, full professional teacher status would be gained with an appropriate advanced qualification in education probably at Masters level (as is the practice in some states in the USA). Each of the three stages would be separated by professional hurdles, and passing on to the next stage would be accompanied by a higher salary.

Such a phased approach to full professional qualification would help to reconcile the conflicts and contradictions described above. It should also be observed that the National Curriculum will, during the 1990s, be placing much greater responsibilities on teachers, not only in the organization and implementation of a highly structured curriculum, but also in its assessment. I suggest that the requirements of Teacher Assessment and Standard Assessment Tasks (SATs) will be such as to be properly the responsibility of professional teachers — not licensed teachers, probationers or those who have just reached Qualified Teacher Status (QTS). (QTS could thereby acquire a nice new meaning — such teachers should only administer National Curriculum Assessment if under the supervision and training of a fully professional teacher.) The logic of this situation would be that all the Masters degrees in Education giving professional teacher status would have to include appropriate courses covering the National Curriculum and its assessment. Thus the core curriculum idea would apply not only to ITT but to an important aspect of INSET.

An appropriate *target* for ITT would be to ensure that all children 11–18 are taught National Curriculum subjects by teachers qualified in that subject (or otherwise certified as competent). For INSET the *target* should be that all teachers should have the opportunity (at least on a part-time basis) to upgrade their professional qualifications to Masters' level. Full-time release is expensive, but part-time courses are available and are extremely good value for employers. They should be encouraged in the ways suggested above.

Adult Education

There is a danger that for the rest of the century the urgent need for training will drive out other kinds of adult education. This is a trap that must be avoided. LEAs should be encouraged to continue to organize adult classes of a non-vocational kind. Here again a voucher system might encourage the survival of the system.

Conclusion: A Note on Educational Theory

One of the more bizarre developments in recent years has been the hostility shown by politicians, particularly those on the right, towards educational theory. In part this is an aspect of the 'amateur' tradition so damaging in industry. Some have suggested that there is too much theory involved in the training of teachers, or even that the theory has a pernicious effect on students who should be spending more time on 'practice'. Others, (including Kenneth Clarke), have blamed 'fashionable theories' for allegedly deteriorating reading standards, or for poor achievements in mathematics. Some have accused colleges of education, polytechnics and University Departments of Education of deliberate indoctrination (Scruton *et al*, 1985).

It may be worth a little space to clarify some of these issues — not least in the hope of engendering greater consensus. First, it has to be stated that with education, medicine or any other kind of professional service it is impossible to have any activity or practice which is free of theory. The theory may be regarded as convention or tradition, or even disguised as common-sense, but unless a response to a problem were completely random it would have to be guided by some set of criteria or principles. Those who claim to teach (or to practise medicine) without theory are either deluding themselves or are using someone's theory without knowing what it is. (Just as Moliere's character discovered one day that he had been speaking prose all his life.) I can remember a good example of this 'theory-free' attitude: I accompanied my wife to the first lesson of a dog training course. The instructor began by telling his class to forget all they had read in books or any other kind of theory — they were just to listen to him. He then proceeded to deliver a series of precepts which were pure behaviourism! Some teachers fall into the same trap, denying the value of any theory whilst showing by their actions (and advice) that they are followers of 'theory' of some kind, involving such practical advice to young teachers as 'don't smile until Christmas'. It is in the interests of all who wish to improve education to promote more and better education research and the development of theory.

The problem with educational theory is that it is relatively under-developed but attempts to deal with issues of great complexity. It is also true that *in the past* some of what was included in initial training courses had little connection with the immediate problems of classroom management and control. If you go far enough back in history, some courses on educational theory consisted of an account of the views of great educators of the past — Plato, Comenius, perhaps ending with Dewey. Such courses were by no means a waste of time, but they were not the highest priority for those whose immediate needs were preparing to face a difficult class the following week. The next main phase in the development of theory courses consisted in identifying contributary disciplines and showing their applicability to education: history of education, philosophy and psychology reigned supreme in the 1950s. And then in the 1960s, especially under the influence of Richard Peters, efforts were made to move away from the isolated disciplines towards 'integration' — bringing theoretical perspectives to bear on educational issues from the point of view of philosophy, psychology and (by now) sociology, with the emphasis on the relevance of these disciplines to the real world of teaching. This was always thought to be very difficult, but sometimes worked very successfully, given adequate rehearsal time by the theorists involved. It tended to work better with practising teachers than with younger students on initial training courses who might still feel that three-pronged attacks on 'indoctrination', 'punishment' or 'intelligence' were not their main worries when they were preparing for teaching practice.

I suppose such approaches to initial training still exist somewhere, but I would not know where to advise anyone to go if they wanted to see that kind of 'theory'. During the 1970s there was a further development which is still being worked out. Attempts began to be made to identify what were the real issues and problems of student teachers on practice in local schools, and to see what light any kind of educational theory could throw on them. Less was heard of psychology, philosophy and sociology, although the same lecturers were likely to be involved, and they did not find the new challenge easy.

Sometimes the issues and problems thrown up for discussion — maybe even solution — were highly contentious. For example, specific problems of dealing with ethnic minority students gave sociologists a marvellous opportunity to theorize about inequality, deprivation, cultural differences and so on, without providing much help to young students having to cope with very difficult classroom situations. (And where, incidentally, they might get very little help from practising teachers either.) It was all very difficult.

A final stage, still being worked out theoretically and practically, derived partly from the work of Donald Schön (1983) in the USA, partly from curriculum theorists such as Laurence Stenhouse (1975), and partly from a change of mind by the philosopher Paul Hirst (1984). They all agreed that the earlier model of identifying good theory and then putting it into practice was basically flawed. Educational theory, like other kinds of practical service such as medicine, was essentially generated out of successful practice. Schön's phrase — 'the reflective practitioner' — is helpful: a good professional teacher, for example, not only does a good job but reflects on what he/she is doing so that he/she can both improve his/her own practice and pass on useful advice to other practitioners who are in training or less experienced or less reflective. Part of this process of reflection might be to enrich practice by theoretical insights derived from other disciplines such as psychology. But a trainee practitioner does not start with the disciplines, he/she starts with the practice.

This is now the dominant approach to educational theory. But it is very difficult, and there are (especially in the USA) many disputes about the meaning of practice, the nature of reflection and so on. Nevertheless, in education and in other professions this kind of approach increasingly provides the basis of 'theory' in ITT and INSET (although for practising teachers it would not be inappropriate for them to study philosophy or psychology as disciplines in their own right, with a view to using them as part of the reflective practitioner process). Most politicians and their advisers who criticize educational theory have very little idea about the changes that have taken place, or indeed of the complexities involved. One of my colleagues did distinguished research in physics before getting involved in science education; he has no doubt that education research is much more difficult than research in physics, and learning to be a good teacher much more complex than becoming a physicist. That view is by no means uncommon. Such areas as curriculum and assessment are extremely complex and difficult to teach. It is very frustrating for teacher educators to be told that it is all common-sense, or that fashionable theories are responsible for under-achievement.

One of the advantages of educational theory backed up by educational research is that results are public and should provide a safeguard against fads and fashions in the teaching of reading or mathematics.

Mistakes of a theoretical kind have occurred in the past, and no doubt will occur from time to time in the future. Young teachers (and probably older lecturers) have misinterpreted or misapplied Rousseau's philosophy, Piaget's psychology or Bernstein's sociology. Some 'loony left' theorists have occasionally suggested that there are more important things in life than learning to read; but they have always been sharply criticized by other educationists and very rarely been taken seriously by practitioners. The exceptions inevitably hit the headlines in the popular press — such as the William Tyndale scandal in 1975. We should also remember that medical theory has in the past advocated such practices as blood-letting and leeches, took a long time to find a theoretical explanation for diseases such as scurvy, and still over-prescribes tranquilizers on a massive scale. This is not say, however, that medical theory is inferior to common-sense or that medical education is a waste of time.

There is another aspect of education theory which should not be forgotten. If it were possible within a course lasting a year or so to produce teachers who were perfectly competent classroom practitioners, there would still be other questions to ask. A good history teacher needs to be able to answer 'Why learn history?' or 'Why learn about the Tudors and Stuarts?'. The answers to such questions cannot be purely utilitarian; they need to be philosophical in a wider sense — and need to include some kind of vision of the sort of society we want to live in. At that stage consensus becomes more difficult: there are no 'correct' answers to some questions, and certain differences of opinion may be irreconcilable. But, bearing in mind the discussion of values in chapter 7, enough consensus can be generated to keep the whole system working.

For some years it looked as though our society was becoming more technocratic and less certain of fundamental values. Recently there has been a significant change: the stress on conservation, pollution of the environment, and the survival of the planet, has caused young people to be much more concerned with more fundamental theoretical questions, and even to ask 'what is it all for?'. In the conflict spirit of the 1980s a 'Thatcherite' answer might have been couched largely in terms of the individual and employment; in the consensus spirit of the 1990s, however, a more acceptable answer would also include much wider references to the quality of life of the whole community. It has sometimes been pointed out that parents can, in one sense, opt out of the state education system by sending their children to private schools. But in another sense no-one can opt out of the system: indirectly we all benefit, or suffer, from the education and training that *all* young people receive at school. In that sense there is no escape; opting out only deals with one immediate, individual aspect of the situation.

That wider perception of education is related to the vision of permanent education or 'a learning society' with which this chapter began. The standards of the state education service are central to the whole question of quality of life for the entire community. There are signs that at last this message is beginning to be understood.

Bibliography

ADAM SMITH INSTITUTE (1983) *The Omega Report*, London, ASI.

ADLER, M., PETCH, A. and TWEEDIE, J. (1989) *Parental Choice and Educational Policy*, Edinburgh, University of Edinburgh Press.

AHIER, J. and FLUDE, M. (Eds) (1983) *Contemporary Education Policy*, Beckenham, Croom Helm.

ALDRICH, R. and LEIGHTON, P. (1985) *Education: Time for a New Act?*, London, Bedford Way Papers **23**.

AULD, R. (1976) *William Tyndale Junior and Infants Schools Report*, London, ILEA.

BAKER, K. (1987) Speech in the House of Commons, *Hansard*, 1 December.

BALL, C. (1990) *More Means Different*, London, Royal Society of Arts.

BALL, C. (1991) *Learning Pays*, London, Royal Society of Arts.

BALL, S.J. (1990) *Markets, Morality and Equality in Education*, London, Hillcole Group.

BANKS, O. (1955) *Parity and Prestige in English Secondary Education*, London, Routledge and Kegan Paul.

BARKER, R. (1972) *Education and Politics*, Oxford, Oxford University Press.

BARNETT, C. (1986) *The Audit of War*, London, Macmillan.

BARR, N. (1987) *The Economics of the Welfare State*, London, Weidenfeld & Nicolson.

BASH, L. and COULBY, D. (Eds) (1989) *The Education Reform Act: Competition and Control*, London, Cassell.

BENEDICT, R. (1934) *Patterns of Culture*, various.

BLAKE, R. (1985) *The Conservative Party from Peel to Thatcher*, London, Fontana.

BOGDANOR, V. (1991) 'Where will the buck stop?', *Times Educational Supplement*, 14 June.

BOYSON, R. (Ed.) (1970) *Right Turn*, London, Churchill Press.

BOYSON, R. (Ed.) (1972) *Education: Threatened Standards*, London, Churchill Press.

BROWN, M., CHOPE, C., FALLON, M. *et al* (1985) *Save Our Schools*, London, Conservative Political Centre.

BUTLER, R.A. (1973) *The Art of the Possible*, Harmondsworth, Penguin.

CACE (1959) *15–18* (The Crowther Report), London, HMSO.

CACE (1963) *Higher Education: A Report* (The Robbins Report), London, HMSO.

CALLAGHAN, J. (1987) *Time and Chance*, London, Collins.

CBI (1989) *Towards a Skills Revolution*, London, Confederation of British Industry.

CHITTY, C. (1989) *Towards a New Education System: The Victory of the New Right?*, Lewes, Falmer Press.

CHUBB, J.E. and MOE, T.M. (1990) *Politics, Markets and America's Schools*, Washington, D.C., Brookings Institute.

CLARKE, K. (1991) speech to the ACFHE, London, DES Press Release, 22 February.

COLERAINE, LORD (1970) *For Conservatives Only*, London, Tom Stacey.

CONSERVATIVE NATIONAL ADVISORY COMMITTEE ON EDUCATION (CNACE) (1974) *Opportunity and Choice in Education*, London, CNACE.

CONSERVATIVE PARTY (1974) *Manifesto*, London.

CONSERVATIVE PARTY (1976) *The Right Approach*, London.

CONSERVATIVE PARTY (1979) *Manifesto*, London.

CONSERVATIVE PARTY (1983) *Manifesto*, London.

COULBY, D. (1989) 'The ideological contradictions of educational reform' in BASH, L. and COULBY, D. (Eds) *The Education Reform Act: Competition and Control*, London, Cassell.

COWLING, M. (Ed.) (1978) *Conservative Essays*, Cambridge, Cambridge University Press.

COX, C. (1988) 'What makes people like us tick?', *Times Educational Supplement*, 16 September.

Cox, C. (1989) 'Unqualified approval', *Times Educational Supplement*, 6 January.

Cox, C. and Marks, J. (1988) *The Insolence of Office*, London, Claridge Press.

Cox, C.B. and Boyson, R. (1977) *Black Paper 1977*, London, Temple Smith.

Cox, C.B. and Dyson, A.E. (Eds) (1969a) *Fight for Education: A Black Paper*, London, Critical Quarterly Society.

Cox, C.B. and Dyson, A.E. (1969b) *Black Paper Two*, London, Critical Quarterly Society.

Crick, B. (1987) *Socialism*, Milton Keynes, Open University Press.

Crosland, A. (1956) *The Future of Socialism*, London, Cape.

Crosland, S. (1982) *Tony Crosland*, London, Cape.

Dahrendorf, R. (1990) *The Strange Death of Socialism* (Gresham Lecture), Dublin, Studies, 79.

Darling-Hammond, L., Wise, A.E. and Pease, S.R. (1983) 'Teacher evaluation in the organisational context', *Review of Educational Research*.

Dean, D.W. (1986) 'Planning for a post-war generation: Ellen Wilkinson and George Tomlinson', *History of Education*, 15.2 pp. 95–117.

Department of Education and Science (1972a) *Education: A Framework for Expansion*, London, HMSO.

Department of Education and Science (1972b) *Teacher Education and Training* (The James Report), London, HMSO.

Department of Education and Science (1976) Yellow Book (unpublished), but in DES Library.

Department of Education and Science (1977) *Curriculum 11–16*, London, HMSO.

Department of Education and Science (1978a) *Curriculum 11–16*, London, HMSO.

Department of Education and Science (1978b) *Higher Education into the 1990s*, London, HMSO.

Department of Education and Science (1981) *Curriculum 11–16: A Review of Progress*, London, HMSO.

Department of Education and Science (1983a) *Curriculum 11–16: Towards a Statement of Entitlement*, London, HMSO.

Department of Education and Science (1983b) *Teaching Quality*, London, HMSO.

DEPARTMENT OF EDUCATION AND SCIENCE (1985) *Better Schools*, London, HMSO.

DEPARTMENT OF EDUCATION AND SCIENCE (1987) *Higher Education: Meeting the Challenge*, London, HMSO.

DEPARTMENT OF EDUCATION AND SCIENCE (1988) *National Curriculum TGAT Report*, London, HMSO.

DEPARTMENT OF EDUCATION AND SCIENCE (1991a) *White Paper: Education and Training for the 21st Century*, London, HMSO.

DEPARTMENT OF EDUCATION AND SCIENCE (1991b) *White Paper: Higher Education: A New Framework*, London, HMSO.

DONOUGHUE, B. (1987) *Prime Minister*, London, Cape.

DYSON, A.E. (1969) 'The sleep of reason' in COX, C.B. and DYSON, A.E. (Eds) *Fight for Education: A Black Paper*, London, Critical Quarterly Society.

EDWARDS, T., FITZ, J. and WHITTY, G. (1989) *The State and Private Education: An Evaluation of the Assisted Places Scheme*, Lewes, Falmer Press.

FARMER, M. and BARRELL, R. (1982) 'Why student loans are fairer than grants', *Public Money*, **2**, 1.

FENWICK, I.G.K. (1976) *The Comprehensive School 1944–70*, London, Methuen.

FINEGOLD, D. *et al* (1990) *A British Baccalaureat*, London, IPPR.

FINEGOLD, D. and SOLSKICE, D. (1988) 'The failure of training in Britain', *Oxford Review of Economic Policy*.

FLEW, A. (1987) *Power to the Parents*, London, Sherwood Press.

FLUDE, M. and HAMMER, M. (Eds) (1990) *The Education Reform Act 1988: Its Origins and Implications*, Lewes, Falmer Press.

FORD, J. (1969) *Social Class and the Comprehensive School*, London, RKP.

FRIEDMAN, M. (1962) *Capitalism and Freedom*, Chicago, IL, University of Chicago Press.

GAMBLE, A. (1988) *The Free Economy and the Strong State*, London, Macmillan.

GIPPS, C. (1989) *Assessment*, London, Hodder.

GOLDSTEIN, H. (1987) *Multilevel Models in Educational and Social Research*, London, Charles Griffin.

HAGUE, D. (1991) *Beyond Universities*, London, IEA Hobart.

HAHN, F. (1988) 'On market economies' in SKIDELSKY, R. (Ed.) *Thatcherism*, London, Chatto & Windus.

HALL, S. and JACQUES, M. (1983) *The Politics of Thatcherism*, London, Lawrence & Wishart.

HALSEY, A.H. (1983) 'Schools of democracy' in AHIER, J. and FLUDE, M. (Eds) *Contemporary Education Policy*, Beckenham, Croom Helm.

HART, P.E. and SHIPMAN, A. (1991) 'Financing training in Britain', *National Institute Economic Review*, 2, May.

HAVILAND, J. (Ed.) (1988) *Take Care Mr Baker*, London, Fourth Estate.

HAYEK, F. (1944) *The Road to Serfdom*, London, Routledge.

HAYEK, F. (1976) *The Mirage of Social Justice*, London, Routledge and Kegan Paul.

HAYEK, F. (1978) *New Studies in Philosophy*, Politics, Economics and the History of Ideas, London, Routledge and Kegan Paul.

HEALEY, D. (1989) *The Time of My Life*, London, Michael Joseph.

HEWITT, P. (1989) *A Way to Cope with the World As It Is*, London, Samizdat, No 6.

HIGGINSON, G. (1988) *Advancing 'A' Levels*, London, HMSO.

HILLGATE GROUP (1986) *Whose Schools? A Radical Manifesto*, London, Hillgate Group.

HILLGATE GROUP (1987) *The Reform of British Education*, London, Claridge Press.

HILLGATE GROUP (1989) *Learning to Teach*, London, Claridge Press.

HIRSCH, F. (1977) *Social Limits to Growth*, London, Routledge and Kegan Paul.

HIRSCHMAN, A.O. (1970) *Exit, Voice and Loyalty*, Cambridge, MA, Harvard University Press.

HIRST, P.H. (Ed.) (1984) *Educational Theory and Its Foundation Disciplines*, London, Routledge and Kegan Paul.

JENCKS, C. (1970) *Education Vouchers*, Cambridge, MA, Cambridge Center for the Study of Public Policy.

JONES, K. (1989) *Right Turn*, London, Hutchinson.

JOSEPH, K. (1976) *Stranded in the Middle Ground*, London, Centre for Policy Studies.

KAVANAGH, D. (1987) *Thatcherism and British Politics*, Oxford, Oxford University Press.

KAVANAGH, D. and SELDON, A. (1989) *The Thatcher Effect*, Oxford, Oxford University Press.

KLUCKHOHN, C. (1962) *Culture and Behaviour*, New York, Free Press Glencoe.

KNIGHT, C. (1990) *The Making of Tory Education Policy in Post-war Britain 1950–1986*, Lewes, Falmer Press.

KOGAN, M. (1989) 'Managerialism in higher education' in LAWTON, D. (Ed.) *The ERA: Choice and Control*, London, Hodder & Stoughton.

LABOUR PARTY (1945) *Manifesto: Let Us Face the Future*, London.

LABOUR PARTY (1958) *Learning to Live*, London.

LABOUR PARTY (1987) *Manifesto: Britain Will Win*, London.

LABOUR PARTY (1989a) *Meet the Challenge, Make the Change*, London.

LABOUR PARTY (1989b) *Children First*, London.

LABOUR PARTY (1990) *Aiming High*, London.

LAUWERYS, J.A. (Ed.) (1945) *The Content of Education*, London, University of London Press.

LAWLOR, S. (1988) *Away with LEAs*, London, Policy Study No **98**, Centre for Policy Studies.

LAWTON, D. (1973) *Social Change, Educational Theory and Curriculum Planning*, London, Hodder.

LAWTON, D. (1980) *The Politics of the School Curriculum*, London, Routledge and Kegan Paul.

LAWTON, D. (1983) *Curriculum Studies and Educational Planning*, London, Routledge and Kegan Paul.

LAWTON, D. (1987) 'What kind of national curriculum?', *NUT Education Review*, **1**, 2.

LAWTON, D. (1989a) *Education, Culture and the National Curriculum*, London, Hodder & Stoughton.

LAWTON, D. (Ed.) (1989b) *The ERA: Choice and Control*, London, Hodder & Stoughton.

LE GRAND, J. (1990) 'Rethinking welfare: A case for quasi-markets?' in PIMLOTT, B., WRIGHT, A. and FLOWER, T. (Eds) *The Alternative*, London, W.H. Allen.

LETWIN, O. (1988) *Privatising the World*, London, Cassell.

MACLURE, S. (1989) *Education Re-Formed* (2nd edn), London, Hodder.

McPHERSON, A. and WILLMS, J.D. (1987) 'Equalisation and improvement', *Sociology*, **21**, 4, pp. 509–39.

MAJOR, J. (1991) speech to the Centre for Policy Studies, London, 10 Downing Street Press Release, 3 July.

MANNHEIM, K. (1936) Ideology and Utopia, London, Routledge and Kegan Paul.

MARQUAND, D. (1990) 'A language of community' in PIMLOTT, B., WRIGHT, A. and FLOWER, T. (Eds) *The Alternative*, London, W. H. Allen.

MAUDE, A. (1968) *Education: Quality and Equality*, London, Conservative Political Centre.

MINISTRY OF EDUCATION (1954) *Early Leaving Report*, London, HMSO.

MORTIMORE, P. *et al* (1988) *School Matters*, London, Open Books.

NATIONAL CURRICULUM COUNCIL (1990) *Core Skills*, York, NCC.

NOZICK, R. (1974) *Anarchy, State and Utopia*, Oxford, Blackwell.

O'HEAR, A. (1988) *Who Teaches the Teachers?*, London, SAU.

O'KEEFFE, D. (1988) 'A critical look at a national curriculum and testing', paper presented to the annual meeting of the American Educational Research Association, New Orleans.

O'KEEFFE, D. (1990) *The Wayward Elite*, London, ASI.

PARKINSON, M. (1970) *The Labour Party and the Organisation of Secondary Education*, London, Routledge and Kegan Paul.

PIMLOTT, B., WRIGHT, A. and FLOWER, T. (Eds) (1990) *The Alternative*, London, W.H. Allen.

POPPER, K. (1963) *The Open Society and its Enemies*, London, Routledge and Kegan Paul.

PRAIS, S.J. and WAGNER, K. (1983) *Schooling Standards in Britain and Germany*, London, NIESR.

PRING, R. (1987) 'Privatisation and education', *Journal of Education Policy*, **4**, 2.

PURKEY, S. and SMITH, M. (1983) 'Effective schools: A review', *Elementary School Journal*.

Quicke, J. (1988) 'The new right and education', *British Journal of Educational Studies*, **26**, 1.

RANSON, S. (1990) 'From 1944–88: Education, citizenship and democracy' in FLUDE, M. and HAMMER, M. (Eds) *The Education Reform Act 1988: Its Origins and Implications*, Lewes, Falmer Press.

Rawls, J. (1972) *A Theory of Justice*, Oxford, Oxford University Press.

ROYAL SOCIETY (1991) *Beyond GCSE*, London, Royal Society.

RUMBOLD, A. (1989) speech to 'A' level conference, London, DES, November.

RUTTER, M. *et al* (1979) *Fifteen Thousand Hours*, London, Open Books.

SAMS, B. (1991) reported in *Education*, **178**, 6, 9 August, pp. 101–2.

SAYER, J. (1985) *What Future for Secondary Schools?*, Lewes, Falmer Press.

SCHÖN, D. (1983) *The Reflective Practitioner*, London, Temple Smith.

SCRUTON, R. (1980) The Meaning of Conservatism, London, Macmillan.

SCRUTON, R., ELLIS-JONES, A. and O'KEEFFE, D. (1985) *Education and Indoctrination*, London, Education Research Centre.

SECONDARY HEADS ASSOCIATION (1991) *The Way Forward*, London, Secondary Heads Association.

SELDON, A. (1986) *The Riddle of the Voucher*, London, IEA.

SEXTON, S. (1977) 'Evolution by choice' in COX, C.B. and BOYSON, R. (Eds) *Black Paper 1977*, London, Temple Smith.

SEXTON, S. (1986) 'Hands off these schools', *The Times*, 18 September.

SEXTON, S. (1987) *Our Schools: A Radical Policy*, London, IEA.

SEXTON, S. (1988) 'No nationalized curriculum', *The Times*, 9 May.

SHERMAN, A. (1987) 'How everyone could have a public school education', *The Daily Telegraph*, 6 August.

SIMON, B. (1991) *Education and the Social Order 1940–1990*, London, Lawrence & Wishart.

SKIDELSKY, R. (Ed.) (1988) *Thatcherism*, London, Chatto & Windus.

SKILBECK, M. (1976) *Culture, Ideology and Knowledge*, Milton Keynes, Open University Press, E203.

SKILBECK, M. (1980) *Core Curriculum for Australian Schools*, Canberra, CDC.

SKILBECK, M. (1984) *School-based Curriculum Development*, London, Harper & Row.

SMITHERS, A. (1990) *Teacher Loss*, Manchester, University of Manchester Press.

SMITHERS, A. and ROBINSON, P. (1991) *Staffing Secondary Schools in the 90s*, Manchester, University of Manchester Press.

STENHOUSE, L. (1975) *An Introduction to Curriculum Research and Development*, London, Heinemann.

STUBBS, W. (1988) 'What hope for London's education service?' in HAVILAND, J. (Ed.) *Take Care Mr Baker*, London, Fourth Estate.

TAWNEY, R.H. (1922) *Secondary Education for All*, London, Allen & Unwin.

TAWNEY, R.H. (1931) *Equality*, London, Allen & Unwin.

TAWNEY, R.H. (1934) *The Choice Before the Labour Party*, Political Quarterly.

WIENER, M. (1985) *English Culture and the Decline of the Industrial Spirit*, Harmondsworth, Penguin.

WHITE, J. *et al* (1981) *No Minister: A Critique of 'The School Curriculum'*, London, Bedford Way Paper.

WILLIAMS, R. (1961) *The Long Revolution*, Harmondsworth, Pelican.

WORSTHORNE, P. (1978) 'Too much freedom' in COWLING, M. (Ed.) *Conservative Essays*, Cambridge, Cambridge University Press.

WRAGG, T. (1988) *Education in the Market Place*, London, NUT.

YOUNG, H. (1989) *One of Us*, London, Macmillan.

Index